# Chambers

## *writing for the web*

**by Susannah Ross**

CHAMBERS
An imprint of Chambers Harrap Publishers Ltd
7 Hopetoun Crescent
Edinburgh EH7 4AY

First published by Chambers Harrap Publishers Ltd
© Chambers Harrap Publishers Ltd 2007

A CIP catalogue record for this book is available from the British Library.

ISBN 978 0550 10324 6

Editor: Ian Brookes
Prepress Controller: Becky Pickard

Designed and typeset by Chambers Harrap Publishers Ltd, Edinburgh
Printed and bound in Spain by GraphyCems

# CONTENTS

## Part Three: Putting it into Practice

# ACKNOWLEDGEMENTS

Thanks to Clare Brigstocke of the BBC who started me training people to write for websites, to Rupert Morris of Clarity who persuaded me to write my first Web writing book, to François Hubert of Cortexte in Montreal who encouraged me to write a second, to Julia Swann of Select Ideas for her kind criticism of the draft and help with the illustrations, and to Sheila Ferguson for her careful proofreading.

I am grateful to the following for allowing me to use their Web pages, many of which have changed since the time of writing, as illustrations:

| | |
|---|---|
| AA | theaa.com |
| Amazon | amazon.com and amazon.co.uk |
| Cancer Research UK | cancerresearchuk.org |
| Charities Aid Foundation | cafonline.org |
| Clarity business solutions in writing | clarity4words.co.uk |
| Dan Cederholm | simplebits.com |
| Dell | dell.com |
| eBay | eBay.co.uk |
| Ford | ford.co.uk |

| Handles Direct | handlesdirect.co.uk |
| Henderson Financial Group | gohenderson.com |
| Marketing Professionals | marketingprofs.com |
| Oxford University | ox.ac.uk |
| UBS | ubs.com |
| Weyerhaeuser | weyerhaeuser.com |

and to Faber & Faber for permission to quote from *The Real Thing* by Tom Stoppard, Eyetools Inc. for permission to use their 'Golden Triangle' image and Mr D C Raitby, owner of The Hardware Shop in Woodstock, for permission to use his shop as an example.

It's the words that matter. Research into how people use the Web repeatedly shows that the words used on a website are crucial to its success. It seems obvious when you think about it. Yet we are so preoccupied with the colour, the design, the links and the layout that the question 'What is the site going to say?' is often the last thing we consider.

Successful sites are those with a clear purpose, clearly expressed. They contain the right amount of information and are well structured and presented. Many websites fail because they have not been properly thought out or carefully written. Now that tracking software can pinpoint the place and time at which a site loses its users, the failures can often be attributed to poorly organized information or unclear writing. And many sites are never found at all because they have not been written in a way that makes them easy for search engines to index.

The Web is a demanding medium for writers. You have a few seconds in which to get the user's interest and you can lose it very quickly; you have to organize your material quite differently from the way you would for a printed publication; and your product is never finished. This *Desktop Guide* will help you understand the medium you are writing for and meet those demands. It will take you through the process of writing for the Web step by step, giving you techniques for tackling individual tasks, useful examples of what works and what doesn't, and a reminder of the basic rules of written English.

Whether you are starting from scratch or maintaining an existing site; whether you contribute to a small part of a site or are responsible for the whole thing, you can keep the *Desktop Guide* by your side and consult it as you need it.

# Part One
# Thinking about
# Websites

# What's so special about the Web?

This chapter describes the characteristics of the Web as a medium. It looks at the way websites work and what that means for writers. These are the ideas that inform the advice in this Desktop Guide.

Look at a book. Then look at the home page of a website on your screen. With the book, the whole thing is there in your hand. One glance at the cover, and the size and shape of it tells you what kind of book it is. You can thumb through more than 150 pages in less than a minute to see whether it is what you want. You are scanning several hundred words a second. If you look for something in particular, it will probably take you a couple of minutes to find and read the words you want.

Compare that with a website such as the one in Figure 1. When you look at the home page, you have no idea how many pages there are and only a vague idea of what sort of site it is. Once you start looking, you can usually see only one page at a time. You may have at most a few dozen words on the screen. It's rather like using a magnifying glass to read a road atlas:

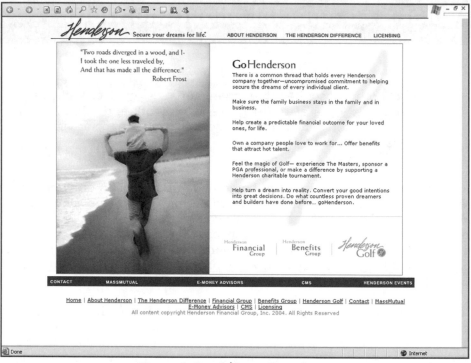

**Figure 1** A website at first glance

you can clearly see only the small part under the glass; you cannot see the whole page, let alone the whole atlas. With a website, you depend on the site itself to tell you where you are and how to find your way around. So the organization of the site and the words it uses to explain itself are crucial. All the more so when you consider that a book is a finite object, whereas a website is potentially infinite. It can grow and change all the time.

A website does not work in straight lines. You may dip in and out of this book, or read the contents in a variety of orders, but it is written with a beginning, a middle and an end. Its pages are numbered in sequence and there is an index at the back. A website has a sort of beginning, in the form of a home page, but there is no guarantee that that's the page you will see first. When you arrive at a page, it has no numerical relationship to the rest of the site. Again, you rely on the site itself to tell you where you are and where you can go next.

All this is by way of explaining why the Web is such a demanding medium to write for. There's more to come. We've had hundreds of years to work out how to write books and less than twenty years to work out how to write for websites. We are still in the early stages of this medium.

### A different medium
The World Wide Web (its full name, hence the common abbreviation www) is part of the Internet, which was originally a United States military

communication network. The World Wide Web was set up in the early 1990s to enable academics to have access to one another's research. It was invented to share information. What made it unique as a medium was the ability to link information from anywhere to anywhere.

Once people were able to read other people's documents on their own computers, they began to think of all kinds of things they could do with people through this new medium. Not only could they share ideas with people in the next room or a continent away, they could make contact and do business with one another in many different ways. The Web is essentially an interactive medium. Relationships – academic, political, personal and commercial – are at its core.

The sharing and the linking, the interactivity, are what make the Web different from other media. Television and radio have become more interactive by using the Web and allowing the audience to participate in programmes. More and more programmes are available on demand through a variety of media including portable devices, computers and television sets. But television and radio are still mainly one-way traffic. The broadcaster decides what you, the viewer or listener, will receive. The programme is linear. Until it has ended, you are unable to see or hear the whole of it, skip the bits that don't interest you or go back to something that was puzzling or particularly pleasing.

When you read a book, magazine or newspaper, you are rather more in control. If you are in a library or bookshop or at a newspaper stand, you can see quite quickly, there and then, what each publication has to offer. You can ask advice and help in finding a particular publication or piece of information. Once you've made your choice, you can decide where to begin, what to skip and what to reread. As a reader of a printed publication you are already more active than when you watch or listen to a broadcast.

Now compare those experiences with using the Web. You go to the Web for a purpose. You want information, to buy something, to ask advice, to exchange views or to make contact with someone. You may want to listen to music or speech. You may want to see some pictures (although the quality may not be as good as on a television set). Besides, you are sitting at a desk using a keyboard. You are active and purposeful. If you want to watch pictures or listen to music, you are more comfortable on the sofa. That is why this *Desktop Guide* calls people who use the Web 'users' – not an 'audience', and not 'readers'.

## A demanding medium

Users are active. They want something. If one site does not give it to them, they have, theoretically, a choice of several hundred million others. The number is growing all the time. More people are getting online and more people are setting up sites. So when you write for a website, you are competing with millions for the attention of the user. What is more, for some users being online costs money. One of the reasons for the rapid growth of Internet use in the United States was that local telephone calls were free. Many users all over the world now use broadband connections. But plenty of users are paying by the minute or blocking a telephone while they are online. Users don't want to waste time. They are demanding and impatient.

They can demand something at any time of day or night. A website has no time of broadcast, time of going to print or day of publication. For the user it exists at the moment that they want it. Because it *can* be changed or updated at any time, users tend to expect that it *will* be. This is another reason why they are impatient.

Once they are in a site, they can choose where to go. They don't necessarily start at the home page. They don't necessarily choose the first link that is offered. They may follow several links or none at all. The possibilities are huge because, unlike a radio programme or a book, a website is non-linear: it does not have a beginning, a middle and an end. This means that on each page the identity of the site must be clear, and the user should be made aware of how the page relates to the rest of the site.

There's another point about how people use the Web. Most people prefer reading on paper in a comfortable chair to reading on a screen sitting at a desk. Not only can you thumb through a book quickly; you can decide where to read it, how to hold it in the best light and what is the right distance from your eyes. Reading on a screen is not a particularly comfortable activity. You have little control over the position of the text or your own position at the desk. As it's not comfortable, it is not a very efficient way of obtaining information.

Then there is the screen itself. You will probably have noticed that screens are wider than they are long. They are short and fat or, in publishing terms, 'landscape'. Yet almost everything we read on paper is long and thin or, in publishing terms, 'portrait'. Reading on screen goes against years of experience of reading in print. Furthermore, compared with paper, the screen is a crude vehicle for words and pictures. The resolution on a screen is much lower than in print. Images – photographs, drawings and so on – are reproduced less precisely than they are on paper, and the same goes for the letters that make up your words.

Finally, when we sit in front of a screen looking for information, we expect to find not just what is in a particular website, but what is in any website that might be relevant. We know the information is out there somewhere and we want it now. It's as if we were to go into a library or shop, click our fingers and expect the right book, newspaper or magazine to fly into our hand, open at the right page. The Web writer has to meet this expectation too, by writing not just for the person using the website at any given moment, but also for potential users searching for the information that is in it.

## Lessons for writers

A website cannot be seen as a whole at one glance. It can be any size.
*Lesson for writers: Your site must be well organized and clearly explained.*

A website does not work in straight lines. It is non-linear. It doesn't really have a beginning, much less an end.
*Lesson for writers: Every part of your site must explain itself and its relationship to the whole.*

The Web is interactive. It is about relationships.
*Lesson for writers: Your writing should be conversational.*

People go to the Web for a purpose. They want something. They are 'users'.
*Lesson for writers: Think of what the user is hoping to get from your site rather than what you want to say.*

There are millions of sites competing for users' attention.
*Lesson for writers: Tell the user what you are offering straight away and be clear about it.*

Being online costs time and, for some people, money. Users are impatient.
*Lesson for writers: Be concise. Don't waste the user's time.*

Reading on a screen is not a comfortable activity.
*Lesson for writers: Make it as easy as possible.*

Screens are not as efficient as paper as vehicles for words or images.
*Lesson for writers: Adapt your writing and presentation to the screen.*

Users expect to find your site through a search engine.
*Lesson for writers: Write in a way that helps search engines index your site.*

# What is your website for?

Before you write anything you should ask yourself, 'Why am I writing this? Who is it for and what is it about?' This chapter deals with the first question and gives you ideas to help you plan your site.

Clear writing is the result of clear thinking. Don't be surprised at the number of stages the *Desktop Guide* suggests you go through before putting finger to keyboard. Resist the temptation to go straight to a screen; get some bits of paper instead. The time you spend thinking, playing with ideas, scribbling and crossing things out will pay dividends later. It's much easier to change something on a piece of paper than on a website.

## Sort out your ideas
Talking to people is a good way of sorting out your ideas. Try them on a few potential users and other people, individually or in a group. You will have to explain your ideas, briefly at first, then in more detail if they ask you questions. If they challenge your ideas, you will have to defend them. Talking about them methodically will help you discard ideas that may not work and rethink others. It may also give you new ones.

## WHAT IS YOUR WEBSITE FOR?

In any writing, you should start by asking yourself three questions: Why am I writing? For whom? and About what? So start with the first one and ask yourself what your website is for. Even if you are working on a site that is not yours alone, thinking about what it is for will focus your writing.

Here are some of the things you may think your site exists to do:

*share ideas with people who have the same interest as me*
*allow people to find out about me or my business at any time*
*sell products*
*get feedback from customers*
*get information and opinions from other people that I can use*
*create a community*
*show that we are accountable to those who fund us*
*make me feel good*
*educate people*
*make my boss feel good*
*communicate with suppliers more cheaply*
*try some exciting animations*
*reduce telephone enquiries*
*persuade people to donate money*

The list could go on and on.

## Limit your ambition

There are many things a website can do, so it is tempting to think of all the things that are possible rather than what is essential to your purpose. Be clear which are the things that matter and be ruthless in eliminating everything else. If you could achieve the same result some other way, do so. Websites are time-consuming. They can be very effective; they may even be fun, but they create a lot of work, so resist the temptation to make your site more complicated than it needs to be.

They also set up expectations. All the more reason for you to be clear about what yours is for and, just as important, what it's not for. Remember the busy user, reading words uncomfortably and in some cases paying by the minute. How irritating to come to a site that describes a wonderful place to hold a party and doesn't tell you how to book it! If you are persuading people to donate money, make sure you enable them to do so. It is better to promise less, and deliver, than to disappoint.

## Clarify your purpose

If you look around the Web, it's not surprising that the most successful sites tend to be those with a clear purpose. The narrower your focus the easier it is. So if your purpose is to sell a specific product, such as books or holidays, to provide people with regular access to a particular kind of news or advice, you have a better chance of making your site work than if you just think you ought to have a website.

# WHAT IS YOUR WEBSITE FOR?

Many people talk about setting up a website or having one. They don't talk often enough about running or managing one. Having a website is not like having a book or film to show people. It is more like having a farm. The question is not so much 'What is in it?' or 'What does it look like', but 'What does it do?' A website can live and grow, provided it is well thought-out to begin with and then well managed. It will flourish if it is used and refreshed and fertilized with new information and ideas. If it is not used, it becomes stale. If the links are not checked regularly they may no longer work, they 'rot'. The site withers and dies. It becomes more of a liability than an asset and you have to start again.

If you are setting up a new site or revamping an existing one, go through these six stages:
1.  Think of all the things you want your site to do.
2.  Write each one on a separate piece of paper.
3.  For each one write down: (i) why you want to do it; (ii) how the site will do it; (iii) why the website will do it better than it's done now; (iv) who will be responsible for it.
4.  Put them in order of importance.
5.  Discard as many as you can.
6.  Describe the purpose of your site in a single line (3-10 words).

You might end up with something like this:

| What? | Why? | How? | Why better on the Web? | Order of importance |
|---|---|---|---|---|
| Make our company more efficient | We want to reduce costs | Deal with suppliers online | Faster and cheaper than telephone and post | 1 |
| Advertise our services | We want more business | Put details and prices online | Millions of users | 4 |
| Get feedback on our products | We want to improve the quality | Use online forms | Easier than writing a letter | 3 |
| Cut calls to the office | Calls waste staff time | Provide information online | Users can get information themselves without involving staff | 2 |

## Checklist

- Spend time thinking before you write.
- Talk to other people to help you sort out your ideas.
- Ask yourself what your site is for.
- Test your ideas against a list of possibilities.
- Be clear in your mind what your site is *not* for: avoid setting up false expectations.
- Answer the question 'What does it do?' in fewer than ten words.
- Think how your site may develop after it is set up and who will do the work.

# Who is it for?

Now we deal with the second question you should ask yourself before you write anything: Who is it for? This chapter helps you establish the kind of words that will most effectively connect with your target user.

Once you've decided what you want your site to do, you need to think who it will do it for. Your site is meant to be useful, but who is going to use it? Is it for people you know, people in your neighbourhood, people all over the country, or people anywhere in the world? What sort of people will they be? Will they be young or old? Will they be male or female? Will they be business people, self-employed people, professionals or students? What is their interest in your site? As potential investors or employees, casual browsers or regular users?

## It takes two to communicate

Writing involves two people, not just one. It is not enough to put an idea into words. You have to be sure that the idea is received by the other person as you intended. It has to evoke the appropriate response. The bulb has to light up, so to speak. In certain kinds of communication, there are formulae for expressing this. On a ship, the traditional response to an order is 'Aye, aye, sir'. Radio communications protocol goes one step further with 'Message received and understood'.

As the Web is an interactive medium, it is important to think about the person on the receiving end and how your website can get the response you hope for. If you want a person to do something as a result of what you write – buy something, write back or tell someone else – try asking yourself, 'What would persuade me to do it?' or 'How would I react to this?' Read out what you have written to someone else and see how they react.

## Connect with your users

At the start of this book I asked you to put yourself in the position of the user and compare the way we use books or listen to the radio with the way we use websites. That's the position you should take as much as possible: looking at the site through the eyes of the user. The way you write depends on who you think is going to find your site useful.

Try it yourself. Take a simple story, for example what you did yesterday, and write two versions of it. Write four sentences to an eight-year-old boy you know and four to a senior figure in your own or some other organization. Compare the words you use in the two versions.

Here is the version I wrote for an eight-year-old:

> I went with some friends from the office to see a play. It was all about a family that was very unhappy. The Mum and Dad and two boys seemed to hate each other and each told awful stories about how bad the others were. We were tired and a bit sad by the end, so we had a pizza to cheer ourselves up before going home.

The version I wrote for an adult is quite different:

> I took some colleagues to see *Long Day's Journey into Night*. Long it certainly was! Who ever imagined that dysfunctional families and drug addiction were modern phenomena? It was brilliantly performed, but a somewhat cathartic experience requiring remedial quantities of refreshment afterwards.

In the case of the child, your purpose is clear: your whole attention is focused on making it easy for him to understand. In the other case, your language is likely to become pompous and the words long. Your purpose is confused: you want to inform, but you also want to impress.

One of the best bits of advice on this aspect of writing appears in the preface to the Plain English Handbook put out by the Securities and Exchange Commission (SEC) in the United States. It is written by the investment expert Warren Buffett, whose company is called Berkshire Hathaway. He says:

> Write with a specific person in mind. When writing Berkshire Hathaway's annual report, I pretend that I'm talking to my sisters. I have no trouble picturing them: though highly intelligent, they are not experts in accounting or finance. They will understand plain English, but jargon may puzzle them. My goal is simply to give them the information I would wish them to supply me if our positions were reversed. To succeed, I don't need to be Shakespeare; I must, though, have a sincere desire to inform. No siblings to write to? Borrow mine: just begin with 'Dear Doris and Bertie'.

What's wrong with jargon? Jargon is a kind of shorthand used by colleagues at work or people engaged in the same activity. It facilitates communication within a group and fosters a sense of belonging. So it may be fine to use jargon if you know that the person you are addressing is one of the group. The problem arises when you are trying to communicate with someone who is not, as in Buffett's example. The SEC's plain English campaign is based on the premise that you should not need to be an insider to understand a company report or a share offer. It is in a company's interest to communicate successfully with investors, and investors need to understand the documents if they are to make informed decisions.

One way of making yourself more sensitive to jargon is to practise drawing up lists of in-words for different groups of people – computer buffs, sports people, musicians, car enthusiasts, gardeners, accountants, and so on. There are two examples in the table below. You can see that jargon words are not necessarily unique to a particular field, but are often common words that have a particular meaning in a particular field.

| Accountants' jargon | Marketing jargon |
| --- | --- |
| asset turnover | differentiator |
| depreciation | fusion brand |
| gearing | platform |
| liabilities | relationship building |
| matching | thought leadership |
| realization | traction |
| relevant cost | proposition |

Look at your lists and decide which words are suitable for the person you are aiming at and which are not. If your site is for people working in a particular field or with a particular interest, the in-words or jargon may help create a sense of community. If your site is not for specialists, one or two in-words may still help establish your credibility. Up to a point, you can carry people with you – they may even be interested in finding out about a word they don't understand – but you have to judge at what point you will lose them.

## Look after your users

What matters is that you keep the user in mind. Your website should be designed from the users' point of view and what they can get out of it, rather than from your point of view and what you want to say. Too many sites, especially organizations' first attempts at putting themselves online, started by saying, in effect, 'Here we are. This is our mission statement, here's a photograph of our chairman and that building is our new headquarters.' Who cares? The first question a user asks of a website is 'What will it do for me?' and your task as a Web writer is to answer that question and every other question you think the user will ask.

Once you focus on your user, you may realize that you don't have just one category of user, but several, and therefore several categories of question to answer. Users interested in investing in your company are asking different questions from users looking for a job, and will probably be very different people. Looking after several categories of user requires you to think of the right words for each and – even more important – to think how you can organize your information to meet their different needs. That is what the next chapter is about.

**Checklist**

- Writing involves two people, not one.
- Your purpose is to get a response from another person.
- Choose your words with that person and that purpose in mind.
- Answer the user's first question, 'What will this site do for me?'
- You may have several categories of user.
- All through the site, write with the user's needs in mind.

This chapter gives you practical advice on how to select and organize the information in your site.

Now that you have clearly defined your purpose and decided who you hope will use your website, you need to work out what they will want to know and how you are going to provide the information. How you organize that information is crucial to the success of your website.

## Where to start

When we imagine a user coming to our website, we usually think of the home page and what it looks like. As writers, we are tempted to think the home page is the most important page and to start our planning there. In fact, the home page is the last thing to think about at this stage and should be the last page that you write. If the home page introduces what your site has to offer, how can you decide what should be in it until you have decided what is going to be in your site, what it's all about?

A website should be organized from the bottom up, not the top down. Think of your website as existing to answer users' questions. So your starting point is your user and his or her questions and needs. The time you spend deciding what information you need to put on your site, and how to organize it, is worth it. Some organizations with successful websites have spent anything from six months to a year or more talking to their users and potential users, finding out what they want and planning how to give it to them, before starting to build the site.

## Generating ideas

One method of generating ideas is to take a sheet of paper and divide it into two columns. On the left side write a list of what your users or customers want, and on the right side a list of the information, skills or products you offer. Then try to connect each item with an item on the other side of the page to see how well they fit. That's one way of making you think of the users' wants rather than yourself and what you do. Don't waste your time offering things that no-one wants. There are too many sites that tell you what they want you to know, rather than what you really want to know.

Another method of generating ideas is to take a sheet of paper and write the central idea of your site in the middle. It may be an event, the unique service you are offering or just the name of your organization. Then put yourself in the position of the person who is going to use the site. Think about what this person is likely to want from you and write down ideas as they occur to you, along lines branching out from the central idea. Some will follow on from one

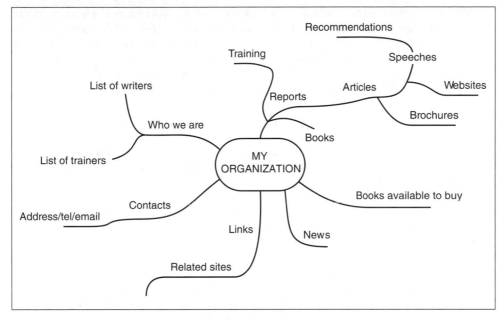

**Figure 2** Generating ideas by association.

another, some will form a new branch from the central idea. When you run out of ideas, stand back and have a look.

Unlike traditional linear notes, this method allows you to see all your ideas at once. Unlike linear notes, it mirrors our natural pattern of thinking, which is by association. Best of all, it works in a similar way to the Web, because of the unique feature of the Web – the link. The link enables users to follow the natural pattern of thinking, so that in the ideal site, when an idea occurs to them, they can follow it by a link. This is what you are aiming for.

If you are working in a group and have access to a whiteboard, so much the better. Then you can brainstorm as a group. The first phase of brainstorming is for generating ideas. Let everyone call out ideas with one person writing them down. Every idea, however off-the-wall, is noted. No-one should question or contradict them at this stage: it's a time for ideas to flow freely. Then you can go through the ideas together, pull them apart, discuss them and agree which to discard and which to keep. The final phase is to put them back together in a structured way: decide which ideas belong together and put them into groups.

A whiteboard is useful for this because it allows you to move ideas around, take them out and put them back, or rewrite them. If you don't have a whiteboard, you may like to use a conventional board with sticky bits of paper. Write each idea on a separate bit of paper and stick it on the board. Then as you discuss the ideas, you can move the bits of paper around, discard them or put them back and finally put them in groups. Bits of ordinary paper on a table or on the floor will do, but pieces of card work better as they are less likely to fly away and are easier to move around a table or carpet.

## Putting them together

When you are organizing, you need to be rigorous. There is so much that can be done on the Web. You can read Einstein's essay on relativity or look at a facsimile of a medieval manuscript as easily as you can book an airline ticket or see tomorrow's weather forecast. It's tempting to think of all the things you can do, rather than concentrating on the least you need to do to make the site work. Think back all the time to what the site is for and reject anything that is not essential to your purpose. This will make your task much easier.

Organizing your material into categories is like creating a filing system. Think how difficult it can be to find things in other people's files, or in unfamiliar supermarkets, and remember: the site is for someone else to use. As the volume of information on the Web grows, so does the need for organizing it in a way that enables users to find what they want. Librarians' skills, far from being threatened with extinction, are valuable and should be much in demand.

The most familiar ways of organizing information are alphabetically, chronologically or geographically. Users will quickly understand a system organized in order from A to Z, or by date or place, and feel comfortable looking for things in it. These systems, however, work best when people know what they are looking for and when there is only one right answer.

Looking for someone's telephone number in a directory is easy as long as you know their name and address. To find an article in a newspaper archive, you need to know the date of publication. Geographical organization also requires some knowledge on the part of the user. Website users don't necessarily know under which letter, date or place they will find the answer to their query. Many come to a site with a general question, a vague idea of what they want, and expect to be offered ways of finding an answer.

Most websites are organized in a more subjective way – by topic, function or user group or a mixture of systems. The Yellow Pages® directory is an example of information organized by topic and then put in alphabetical order, and many websites are similarly organized into categories of products or services. Other sites are organized by function, according to what users might want out of the site – to browse, to buy, to find a local supplier or find out more about the company, as in Figure 3. If organizing by user group is more suitable for your site, you might think of your likely users and put them into categories, as for example a company might divide potential clients into individuals and institutions, while also offering information likely to be of interest to all users, as in Figure 4.

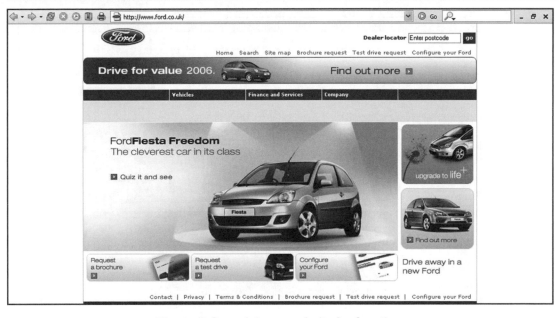

**Figure 3** Organizing a website by function.

**Figure 4** Organizing a website by user group.

Using a mixture of systems enables you to cater for different types of user, and by providing different ways of reaching the same information, you increase the chances of any one user finding what they want. If you organize your information by both user group and topic, for example, a mixture of systems enables you to present the user with a lot of options immediately, as in Figure 5.

## Structure and navigation

At this point you need to think about the hierarchy of information. This may sound like a contradiction of what we said on page 8 about the Web being non-linear – and in this chapter about generating ideas by association instead of linear notes – but one of the key considerations in organizing a website is how easily users can get what they want. You can practise for this by imagining a particular user, creating a character and a scenario for them, then testing your organization of the information to see how well it works.

For example, on a site selling widgets, the user will want to know very soon how much they cost and how to get them. Who makes them is of little interest if they are made in a factory. If, on the other hand, they are individually made in some traditional way, the personality of the craftsman may be a selling point and should be high up the hierarchy. If your site is offering a service, the qualifications of the people providing it are important; the cost may be less of a consideration. If your site is about an event, then how to get there is one of the first things the user will want to know, and so on.

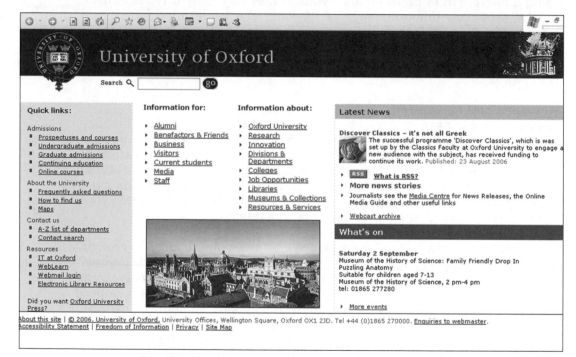

**Figure 5** Using two ways of organizing information.

Many sites are based on the principle that users should be able to find what they are looking for in no more than, say, three clicks. The theory is that if they don't get what they want in three clicks from the home page, they'll go elsewhere, and therefore sites should be organized in a broad and shallow, rather than narrow and deep, structure. In practice, however, users often go through more than three clicks. Research suggests they are happy to do this provided they feel they are making progress, and that in turn depends on their feeling they understand the site and have confidence in it.

If you apply the three-click rule too rigorously, you may present the user with too many options on the home page, causing confusion; and too much information after the third click, causing irritation. I prefer to stress the importance of labelling the pages and sections of your site in a way that makes sense to users and giving them as much information as they need, and no more than they need, at any stage.

Building your site from the bottom up means deciding what the individual pages will be, grouping them together into categories or sections and grouping those categories in turn into bigger sections until you reach the home page. How are you going to enable users to find what they want from the home page? The key is in the way you label the information at each level.

To take a simple example, if at the bottom of your hierarchy you have an article about snoring, that page will be labelled 'Snoring'. The page goes into a category of articles which you might label 'Sleep disorders' and 'Snoring' will be one of the links on the main page of that category. Sleep disorders belong with other disorders that come under the label 'Medical problems' and 'Medical problems' becomes one of the links in your main navigation.

When thinking how to lead the user through a series of choices to what they want, I use the analogy of food. The users are looking for a meal – the full text of an article – but don't want to waste time on any food they don't like. On the home page, you provide a whiff of what's on offer – the main navigation. One level down, you provide a taste – headlines telling them what's in that section. On the next level, a bite – a summary of each article in the subsection – which enables them to click on the one that interests them and read the full text. I go into writing summaries, headlines and links on pages 152–60.

It means a lot of work, but there is no point having lots of useful articles or products on your site if the user can't find them. It is frustrating and time-wasting to come to a long list of items and have to try several in turn to see whether they are what you are looking for. The grouping under headings and the brief, well written descriptions are what make a site work. You may ask why you need to do this when you can have a search button on the home page. The problem with relying on search is that it doesn't necessarily produce satisfactory results. Also, some people don't like to use search, and others are not very good at using it. Finally, knowing that users can search may encourage you to be lazy and think you can just put up information in any form and let the user find it somehow.

When grouping your information into categories, you should aim to have between three and seven items at any one level. Fewer than three isn't a list. More than seven items is hard to take in. If you find your list of options getting longer than seven, either divide the options again or arrange them in a way that quickly becomes obvious, for example using alphabetical order.

### Chunks and links

You should divide your information into discrete chunks – bits that make sense on their own and do not repeat information that appears elsewhere. Your site will be easier for the user to understand if one page is about one topic and contains all the information on that topic. The great thing about the Web is that having arranged your information in a hierarchy, you can still have a link straight from level 2 to something on level 4. You can, for example, offer the user the chance to go straight to buying your widget or the opportunity to find out more about it before deciding. It is particularly important that a user can link to a page containing your organization's contact details from any page in the site.

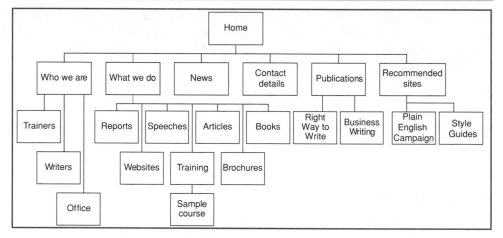

**Figure 6** Hierarchy of information on a website.

There can be two or more ways of getting to the same chunk. For example, you might have a conference that could be found from a list of dates, a list of places or a list of topics. Remember the ideal website, in which whenever an idea or a question occurs to the user, there will be a link to follow. When you describe the conference and mention a speaker, there should be a link to a page about him or her. The better you divide your information into chunks, the easier it will be for you to put links where they are needed because every page or section will make sense on its own, wherever the user links from.

Saying that the same information should not appear in different places does not mean you do not repeat key ideas. On the contrary, the name of your site and what makes it special should appear often to reinforce your message and maintain the identity of the site. Your main navigation, or at least a link to the home page, should appear on every page so that the user never feels lost.

Even if you don't organize the site yourself, being aware of the structure will help your writing. Realizing what it's like to come to a site without any idea of what is in it makes you think about how you can explain the site to the user. Knowing what is in it makes you write your text with the possible links in mind and makes the site both richer and more coherent.

### Where will it go from here?

One further thing to bear in mind when you organize the information on your site is how the site is going to develop. By writing this chapter I have made clear that I believe organization, structure and navigation are editorial responsibilities, an integral part of writing, rather than something to be left to the designer or the coder. Too often the writer is brought in when all the important decisions have been taken, presented with a site that has already been designed and coded, and asked to fill in the spaces.

A site made in this way is likely to be more difficult to develop than one where the writer or editor has been involved from the start. A designer wants to make a website look as good as possible, but websites never look as good as printed documents. They inevitably involve a compromise between what looks good and what works on the screens of individual computers. A beautifully arranged set of five links may be ruined when your business expands and you want to add a sixth. You need to think ahead and ensure that the way the site is organized, and designed, is sufficiently flexible to allow it to grow.

## Checklist

- Spend as long as you can planning your content to meet users' needs.
- Discard any functions that are not essential.
- Organize your site from the bottom up: the home page comes last.
- Plan your hierarchy.
- Test your plan by imagining a user going through your site.
- Divide information into discrete chunks.
- Label your chunks to provide the links on the level above.
- Allow users to navigate the site in different ways.
- Organize your site in a way that allows it to grow.

# The language of the Web

The language of the Web

This chapter talks about good writing in any context as writing which does its job. It looks at the kind of language that works on a website and the differences between written and spoken English. It briefly discusses style.

Good writing is writing that does its job. It achieves its purpose; whether that is to tell you how to operate a lawn mower, to persuade you to book a holiday or to move you to tears over the suffering of a person you don't even know. On a website, we are mainly concerned with the first two types of writing rather than the third. The point of mentioning the third is to stress that writing is always functional.

## Inclusive language

Language is a tool. Its function is to enable people to deal with one another. Just as it can reinforce a sense of community, it can also be used to enable some people to communicate at the expense of others. Children do it all the time. They invent languages to draw a boundary between themselves and grown-ups or other children. Groups in society use words to draw boundaries between themselves and others. They recognize certain words as defining the class or group people belong to. If you use these words, you're in; if you use those words, you're out. As soon as the in-words are taken up by the outsiders, the code is changed; for the purpose of the in-language is not to communicate with outsiders, but to exclude them.

On the Web, you don't want to use a special language that only a few people can understand, nor is it a good idea to use words in a way that is peculiar to your site. There are already plenty of new words that people have had to learn in order to use the Web. For most websites, you want to write in a way that as many people as possible will understand. In any context, good writing is writing that is immediately understandable. It should not need to be read more than once. On the Web – which is a highly competitive environment – poor writing may simply mean the end of the communication. The user will give up and go elsewhere.

### Restricted vocabulary

There has been a rapid convergence of terminology on the Web as the number of users has grown. In the early days every site was different; every site had its own navigation, almost its own language. There were relatively few sites. People had to be technically competent to use the Web at all and they were prepared to work at understanding each site. No more. In a very short time, users have got used to headings like 'About us' and terms like 'shopping basket'. If you thought that 'shopping bag' might be more appropriate for your customers, you would have to weigh up the value of making your site appear more upmarket against the potential loss of customers who didn't recognize 'bag' as having the same function as 'basket'. With millions of sites and everyone expecting to use them, users are not going to bother with a site that does not explain itself well and uses words differently from other sites.

There is nothing new in this. In the early seventeenth century, two works that have had a tremendous influence on the English language were written: Shakespeare's plays and the King James Bible. Both were published at a time of extraordinary growth in the language, yet one has a vocabulary that is twice as rich as the other's.

Their functions were different. The Bible was for instruction. It was written by a rather conservative committee and was intended to be understood and learned by as many people as possible. Repetition of a relatively small number of words suited its purpose. Shakespeare's purpose, on the other hand, was to stimulate the imagination by conjuring up scenes and characters in different periods of history and different countries, real and imagined. He deliberately used new words, and as many as he could, to fulfil his purpose. It didn't matter that not everyone understood every word. In the number of words it uses, the Web is at the King James Bible's end of the spectrum, rather than Shakespeare's.

Restricting the vocabulary makes the medium easy to operate. Most of what you write on a website is there to explain the site to users and enable them to act on what you tell them. You should decide on the terms you are going to use and stick to them. For example, will you ask users to 'join', 'subscribe', 'register' or 'become a member'? If you use more than one term, they may dither. Web writers are in a similar position to technical writers in the need to restrict their vocabulary. Technical writers often work within strict guidelines, such as a list of approved definitions of words, to ensure that their documents are unambiguous. Creative writers, on the other hand, try hard to find different ways of saying the same thing, to avoid repeating themselves. But on the Web, where users are so easily confused, a certain amount of repetition is a virtue.

### Multi-functional writing

Whereas writers in print – whether technical or creative – mostly write for a single purpose, writers on the Web soon realize that what they write may have to serve several purposes at once. So the words you will write for the user to read on the page should also help search engines find your site. The alternative ('alt') text on your images is intended to allow blind or partially sighted users to understand your site using a screen reader, but it can be read by sighted users and is also picked up by search engines. The title text that you write for each page is seen by the user at the top of the screen and picked up by search engines, but also becomes the label used by a browser when users bookmark your page or enter it into their list of favourites.

The need to serve several purposes with the same words, added to the need to restrict the vocabulary, suggests to some people that the language of the Web has to be a dull, repetitive compromise. I prefer to see writing for the Web as a challenge that requires a lot of thinking and planning, as well as skill in choosing words.

## Appropriate words and phrases

If you have bought anything from the website Amazon, you may have noticed amazon.com uses an American term 'shopping cart', whereas its British counterpart amazon.co.uk uses 'shopping basket'. Amazon recognizes that it has different audiences or markets and takes the trouble to use terms appropriate to each.

You may find that your site is aimed at more than one audience and wonder how you can write appropriately for each. If you have organized your site into distinct areas for different audiences you can adapt the language you use to each audience. You may use more technical language in one part of the site and more informal, chatty language in another; but you need to judge how far you can go. You want users to feel that your site, or a particular part of it, is meant for them; on the other hand you do not want your site to lose its identity. Credibility is a vital component in the success of a website. When anyone can set up a website, and so many people abuse the Web for commercial, political or personal gain, it is important that users trust you and believe what you say. You don't want to sound as though you are saying different things to different people.

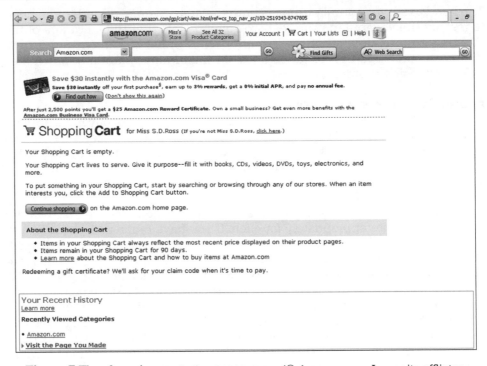

**Figure 7** The shopping cart at amazon.com. (© Amazon.com, Inc. or its affliates. All rights reserved.)

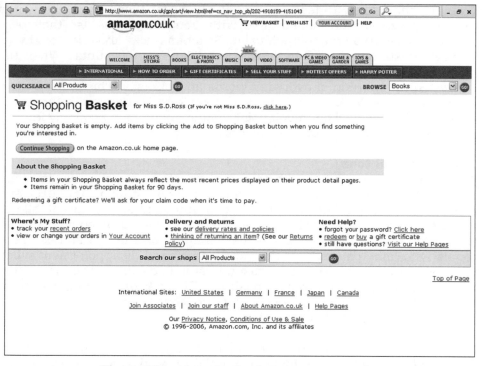

**Figure 8** The shopping basket at amazon.co.uk.

Users are more likely to feel your site is meant for them if you use words they recognize and are comfortable with. Too many sites use their own language rather than that of their users. So a bank talks about its 'products' when its customers probably think about 'loans' or 'accounts'. When the words of successful communicators are analysed, it turns out that they use a very high proportion of everyday words and phrases. This is even more important on the Web where you want people to find your site through a search engine. There's not much point talking about your 'economy fares' if most people are looking for 'cheap flights'.

## Conversational tone

The Web was set up to share things. As well as enabling us to share information, it allows us to do business, pursue common interests and create communities. Because the Web is interactive, because it allows conversations that are almost real, its language should be conversational. The conversation, however, is not real. Think of all the sad stories about people who 'met' on the Internet and then suffered disappointment when they met in reality. Think of all the misunderstandings and even crises within an organization caused by emails misfiring. That's because people write as if they are having a conversation and forget that the vital ingredient of a conversation – the other person – is missing.

This is the crucial difference between written and spoken English, and it is worth spending some time thinking about it. When we have a conversation with someone, we are far more influenced by their physical appearance, their facial expression, attitude and the way they move, their tone of voice and manner of speaking, than we are by the words they use. The words themselves account for about 10% of the communication between us. Try it yourself. How do you feel if someone says she really cares about you, while staring through the window at something going on outside? Imagine seeing television pictures of two groups of men shaking their fists at each other and looking furious, with a commentary saying 'the conciliation talks have been successful.' Which do you believe, what you see or what you hear?

There was a striking example of the power of visual information in the 1960 US presidential election. The candidates, Richard Nixon and John Kennedy, debated the issues on television. Their speeches were also broadcast on the radio. Afterwards the audiences were asked which candidate had won the debate. The radio listeners gave it to Nixon, the television viewers to Kennedy. The television viewers were apparently swayed by Kennedy's clean good looks compared with Nixon's sweaty unshaven face. Kennedy looked confident, Nixon looked shifty. The words were overpowered.

The way we speak conveys an enormous amount of meaning. Think of how many different ways you can say a simple sentence like 'You know'. Depending on the context, your attitude, your gestures, tone of voice and volume you can make those words a statement of fact, a question, a threat, a declaration of love, an exclamation of astonishment, the punchline of a joke, and so on. If you describe someone as 'quite reliable', you can by your tone of voice say either that the person is reliable or that he is not. Without the physical presence of the speaker, words have to work very hard to convey meaning accurately.

Without the physical presence of the other person, the listener or reader, communication can easily go awry. If you tell a joke and no-one laughs, you get your feedback straight away. When you speak to someone you soon know whether you are retaining their interest and whether your message is getting through as intended. If they look bored or puzzled you can change pace, change the subject, ask them a question or try it again a different way. When you write, none of these options is open to you. The words have to do it all.

Spoken English has many subtle ways of distinguishing words, which narrow down the possible options in the listener's mind. We stress some words differently according to how they are used in a sentence. So 'produce' used as a noun is *prod*-uce and used as a verb is pro-*duce*. Sometimes we stress the same word differently when it has different meanings – an 'in-*val*-id pass' does not mean the same as an '*in*-val-id pass'. We pronounce 'the' differently depending on whether it introduces a word beginning with a consonant or a vowel – 'the book' or '*thee* article'. These differences are a great help to anyone listening to spoken English, but unavailable to anyone reading written English.

There are conventions about what we can and cannot say in writing as opposed to speech. For example, it is said that a contraction like 'couldn't', which is normal in speech, should always be replaced by 'could not' in writing. Some publications follow that rule, others don't. This *Desktop Guide* uses contractions, except where the full words provide the right emphasis, in order to sound conversational. Any such convention is, or should be, designed to help your written English make up for the 90% of communication that is missing when the person you are communicating with is not present.

Your Web writing should sound conversational. Even though it is not intended to be read aloud, it should sound good. You will choose one word rather than another because it sounds better as you read it to yourself. You may write 'jail' rather than 'prison', not because of any difference in meaning between the two words, but because one syllable suits the rhythm of the sentence better than two. One reason great literature is great is that it was mostly written to be read aloud. One reason bad writing is bad is that the writer hasn't bothered to listen to it.

## Polished writing
While the tone of your words should be like a conversation, the text that appears on a website must be as good as in a magazine. Your words may be on the screen for a few minutes before you rewrite them or they may be printed out, shown to a lot of people and then kept. Either way, they must look good. Your website is an expression of yourself, your community or your organization. It affects the way you are perceived. So it is worth

spending time ensuring that the writing is as clear, correct and polished as you can make it.

In this chapter I've shown you some of the ways in which writing for the Web is so demanding. You are writing for different audiences, yet trying to make your language inclusive. You are writing for two or three different purposes at once. You are writing as if in a conversation, but without the other person; at the same time you are expected to write as if for a magazine. Because users are impatient and easily confused, you need to aim for absolute consistency in your use of language.

## Style

Before I go on to help you meet these demands, we need to deal with the question of style. You may be wondering what style of writing you ought to adopt for the Web. Don't – or at least don't spend time worrying about it. If you adopt a style that does not come easily to you, you are unlikely to write well. If you are concerned about how you are coming across, you are unlikely to come across well. If you are thinking about yourself, rather than the person you are writing for and what you are writing about, you are putting an obstacle in the way of your purpose in writing. The Victorian poet Matthew Arnold had this reassurance for writers:

> People think I can teach them style. What stuff it all is! Have something
> to say, and say it as clearly as you can. That is the only secret of style.

## Checklist

- Writing is always functional: the language you use depends on your purpose.
- On the Web, you usually want to communicate with as many people as possible.
- Using a limited number of words consistently makes a website easy to operate.
- Your words may serve two or three functions at once.
- You may be writing for more than one audience.
- Everyday words are usually the most effective.
- Your writing should sound conversational.
- The words have to work hard because the other person is not there.
- The writing must be polished.
- Your purpose will determine your style.

**Part Two
Thinking about
Writing**

# Using as few words as possible

The first rule of Web writing is to be concise. Here are some questions and guidelines to help you use only as many words as you need.

Every word on a website must justify itself. The space on a screen is limited, you have very little time to get your message across and the user is impatient. Your aim should be to say what you have to say in as few words as possible.

## Have you thought it through?
One reason people use too many words is that they haven't really thought about what they want to say. So they waffle. Thinking about the three questions, 'Why am I writing?', 'For whom?' and 'About what?', will help you avoid over-writing. We have already discussed the purpose of your writing and the person or people you are writing for. We'll now deal with the third element – the subject matter.

Think of all the times you have had to read something several times to understand it, or perhaps never to understand it at all. The chances are that the writer didn't fully understand it either. You can't hope to put information across to someone else if you haven't digested it yourself. Think of the occasions you have found something difficult to write. The chances are that your source material was hard to understand or there was some information missing or you just hadn't done enough work on it. Consciously or unconsciously, you are not happy writing about something you don't fully understand yourself. Once your thoughts are clear, you can set about choosing the words that express them accurately.

## Are you sure what that word means?

Another reason people use too many words is that they are not sure of their meaning. It's a good idea to keep a dictionary by your side and check that words mean what you think they do. Using words precisely is like having a range of sharp tools at your disposal. Not only are they sharp but each is appropriate to a particular purpose. You would not have much confidence in a plumber who told you he only had a couple of tools and they worked all right on most pipes. Too often we rely on a few expressions to cover most eventualities and end up describing none of them effectively. 'Issue', for example, has become an all-purpose word used for anything from an international crisis to a vaguely uncomfortable feeling. Calling something 'nice' tells us nothing about it, except that we like it.

In his play *The Real Thing*, Tom Stoppard likens good writing to making a cricket bat:

> This thing here, which looks like a wooden club, is actually several pieces of particular wood cunningly put together in a certain way so that the whole thing is sprung, like a dance floor. It's for hitting cricket balls with. If you get it right, the cricket ball will travel two hundred yards in four seconds... What we're trying to do is to write cricket bats, so that when we throw up an idea and give it a little knock, it might travel.

The same character goes on to describe words as:

> ... innocent, neutral, precise, standing for this, describing that, meaning the other, so if you look after them you can build bridges across incomprehension and chaos. But when they get their corners knocked off, they're no good any more...

In order to understand one another, we have to agree about the meaning of words. This is more, not less, vital in a medium that works so quickly, where people expect the message to be immediately clear. You can't afford to be like Humpty Dumpty in Lewis Carroll's *Through the Looking-Glass*:

> 'When I use a word', Humpty Dumpty said, in a rather scornful tone, 'it means just what I choose it to mean – neither more nor less.'

The meanings of words change and new words are introduced into the language all the time. You need to be alert to the way the language is developing. Listen to how people speak, read as much as possible and look at other sites to see how they are using words. When it comes to the essential functions of your site, conformity is a virtue.

## Is that word necessary?

After laziness in preparation, we come to laziness in writing. This is a third reason why we tend to write too much. We are all guilty of tautology – saying the same thing twice – and pleonasm – using unnecessary words. We talk of a 'serious crisis' as though there might be one that didn't matter or a 'complete surprise' as though there were shades of surprises. When writing, we need to go through the words we have chosen to make sure every one is needed.

Look at these phrases. You've probably heard them often, but when you look at them carefully you can see that they are saying the same thing twice.

> *free gift*
> *past history*
> *future prospects*
> *we are all unanimous*
> *attempt to try*

We often, especially in speech, put in words that add nothing to the meaning of what we are saying. Again, if you look critically at such phrases you can cut out the unnecessary words.

*meet up with*
*merge together*
*test out*
*crisis situation*

The following passage contains many words whose meaning is already expressed by other words or phrases. It is verbose. Test your editing skills by seeing how many words you can cut out. You should be able to get rid of at least 20.

Setting up your website involves co-operative collaboration between the various members of a team, such as the designer and the commissioner, for example. The method is a simple one.

Pre-planning is an essential requirement. A practical manual is a helpful support and meeting on a daily or weekly basis is also good practice. Only one person should be in charge, but each member of the team, however, must necessarily be kept informed at every single stage of the project. If not, it can otherwise completely break down.

Undue haste in launching your website should be strongly resisted. Seeing the empty space where your website should be may tend to lead to anxious concern. That is as nothing compared with the horrific nightmare of a website that does not work well.

Here is my version of the same passage. I managed to cut it from 130 words to 101:

> Setting up your website involves collaboration between the members of a team, such as the designer and the commissioner. The method is simple.
>
> Planning is essential. A manual is helpful and meeting daily or weekly is also good practice. One person should be in charge, but each member of the team must be kept informed at every stage of the project. If not, it can break down.
>
> Haste in launching your website should be resisted. Seeing the space where your website should be may lead to concern. That is nothing compared with the nightmare of a website that does not work.

### Is there a simpler way of saying it?

A fourth reason for writing too much is that people use a phrase rather than a single word to say what they mean. Why use the phrase 'make adjustments to' when you can use 'adjust'?

Have a look at these examples:

| despite the fact that | although |
| give an undertaking | undertake |
| in the event that | if |
| in the vicinity of | near |
| make an application | apply |
| make use of | use |
| on a regular basis | regularly |
| serves to explain | explains |

It's almost as if people are frightened of the true meaning of words. Perhaps asking someone to 'co-ordinate arrangements for a party' does make the task sound less daunting than 'arranging' it, but there is no difference in meaning. Certainly politicians and others often use language to obscure reality, but on a website you are trying to communicate clearly and concisely.

Test yourself by finding a single word that conveys the same meaning as the italicized phrases:

We *have absolute confidence in our ability to* deliver this by Monday.
He *came to a decision* to buy the shares.
I am writing to you *with regard to* your proposal.
He was unable to be at the wedding *owing to the fact that* he had broken his leg.

## Are you really trying to inform?

A fifth reason for writing too much is the desire to impress rather than inform. We seem to think it's rude to write briefly, as though words were presents and our reader deserved lots of them. More likely we think that a long letter, report or article shows how much effort we have put in. The opposite is true. It takes far more effort to write concisely, because you have to think and plan, and choose and edit your words. Why should your reader have to wade through three times as many words as necessary? The French philosopher, Blaise Pascal, acknowledged the selfishness of long-winded writers when he apologized at the end of a letter to a friend:

> I have made this longer than usual, only because I have not had the time to make it shorter.

Using few words may sometimes seem abrupt, but if they are the right ones, how powerful they can be! When the Quaker William Penn was arrested and imprisoned for holding a meeting in the street in 1670, he appealed to his father for help. He began his letter 'Because I cannot come, I write.' In our century, think how long a company takes, and how much money it spends, to come up with an advertising slogan of perhaps three words. Those three words may be worth millions of pounds.

## Is every word working?

When you have succeeded in avoiding or overcoming all five causes of verbosity, there is a journalist's device that you can use to go through your words again and pare them to the minimum: it's called the Fish Shop Test. Imagine going to a fish shop. There are fish laid out on the slab in the window. On the window is a notice, 'Fresh Fish Sold Here'. What information does it give you? None that you do not already have. You wouldn't expect the fishmonger to be in business if he was selling stale fish. So you can get rid of 'Fresh'. You can see the 'Fish' in the window so you know that's what his business is. He's certainly not giving it away, so you don't need 'Sold', or 'Here' because it is obviously a fish shop.

Some Web guides argue that using the word 'click' on a Web page is like putting a notice on a shop door saying, 'Depress handle, push door and walk in'. That may be going a bit far when you think how many people still need help finding their way around a website. But it is good practice to test every word you use, to make sure it is adding value, not saying something that is already obvious. For the fishmonger, it might have been 'Harry welcomes you' or 'Lobsters every Thursday in June'.

A shop is a good metaphor for a website, so here's another shop example. There's a hardware shop in Woodstock in Oxfordshire that has a notice above the door saying 'Service with a Snarl'. It's a useful shop, the owner is helpful and you nearly always find what you are looking for. So the shop does what you expect, but the notice is intriguing. It makes you look twice at the shop and remember it. That is a good example of using words to add value.

**Checklist**

- Before you write, think about what you want to say.
- Be sure you understand what you are writing about.
- Choose words that express your meaning exactly.
- Use words that everyone will understand.
- Cut out unnecessary words.
- Use a single word rather than a phrase if you can.
- Check that every word is working.

# Choosing the right words

This chapter starts with the kinds of words you should avoid if you want to be clear and concise. Then it looks at the kinds of words you should be using, and how to improve bad writing.

## What to avoid
### i. Jargon and slang
Avoid jargon because it excludes. It is a language for insiders. It has a useful function within a group or an organization as a kind of shorthand that enables people to communicate easily about what they are doing, but it can also be used to show off knowledge, wealth or social standing for the sole purpose of making the other person feel inferior. If you want to communicate with as many people as possible, don't use it.

Avoid slang for the same reasons. Slang is mostly used by people who know one another, who share the same culture and are of the same age group. Again, unless you are sure that you want to communicate exclusively with those people, avoid it.

## ii. Abbreviations

The need to condense text messages into a limited number of characters has produced some imaginative abbreviations, such as 'GR8' for 'great' and 'CU' for 'see you'. A few of these short forms are understood by most people. Something similar happened after the telegraph was invented in the nineteenth century, especially when telegrams, and later telex, were the main medium for journalists to transmit their stories to their editors. Because transmission was expensive, they became adept at condensing their messages, finding short words like 'bid' instead of 'attempt' and running words together, as in 'upcoming' instead of 'coming up'.

Just as some of these journalists' terms found their way into the newspapers and general use, some texting terms pop up in written English. Some people do not regard them as proper English and may not take seriously a website that uses them. A more important question is whether they are understood by everyone who needs to understand them. If your life depended on an SOS message being understood, you would probably spell out the words rather than use abbreviations. When you are writing for a worldwide medium, rather than friends or colleagues, you want to look professional and be understood by all, so it's better to be cautious and leave this sort of abbreviation to text messages.

Abbreviated names like 'FCO' (Foreign and Commonwealth Office) or 'FSA' (Financial Services Authority) are useful to save space, though they will not necessarily be familiar to everyone. So if you use them, make sure you explain them at least once on every page. Some other abbreviations, such as 'HTML', are nearly always used and understood in their abbreviated form. Most people don't need to know the full name, HyperText Markup Language; they only need to know that it's the code that produces Web pages.

### iii. Terms that exclude

Words that may not constitute jargon or slang may still be exclusive. In order to communicate we have to assume some common points of reference, but we can take this too far. A website that asks you for your zip code assumes it is talking to people in the United States. It makes people outside the United States feel it is not meant for them, even though they might be interested in the content.

Since one of the strengths of the Web is that it can bring people together regardless of where they are, it makes sense to try to make the language we use as inclusive as possible. Even within one country, we make a lot of assumptions about shared experiences and values. A forecast of rain may be welcome to farmers and unwelcome to holidaymakers. People don't all know the same music, read the same books, watch the same television programmes or do the same things to amuse themselves on a Sunday; and this sentence makes several cultural assumptions, including the assumption that everyone takes Sunday off. It comes down to thinking about the person you are aiming your site at and choosing the appropriate words.

### iv. Clichés

Clichés are yesterday's inspirations. The phrase 'over the moon' is wonderfully expressive of joy. It conjures up the picture of the cow jumping over the moon in the nursery rhyme 'Hey Diddle Diddle'. The first time it was used it must have been very effective. The hundred-and-first time, it doesn't impress. It suggests that the person who uses it has not thought, has not chosen his words himself but has pulled something ready-made off the shelf. The writer George Orwell described hackneyed prose as consisting 'less of words chosen for the sake of their meaning, and more ... of phrases tacked together like the sections of a prefabricated henhouse.'

Metaphors such as 'over the moon' and similes such as 'like the sections of a prefabricated henhouse' communicate an idea by creating a picture in the reader's mind. This is what all good writers try to do, but whereas the henhouse is original, 'over the moon' is not. Every word you write should be individually chosen to do its job. George Orwell died long before websites were invented, but as the greatest exponent of clear, simple English in the past century he still has a lot to say about good writing in any medium.

### v. Long, pompous words

The English language is so rich in words that you often have a choice between a short, pithy word and a long, cumbersome one that has the same meaning. The short, pithy one will usually be of German origin, having come into English via the Anglo-Saxons or Danes, and the long, cumbersome one will usually have come from Latin or French, thanks mainly to the Church and the French spoken by the Norman kings and barons. You can guess why people choose the long words. Latin was for so long the language of the educated and the powerful and the habit dies hard. We still, subconsciously even, want to show that we can talk like the elite.

Compare the words from the two different roots:

| Latin origin | German origin |
|---|---|
| adjacent | next |
| assistance | help |
| facilitate | make easy |
| illumination | light |
| inform | tell |
| prior to | before |
| requirements | needs |
| subsequent | later |

Having in effect two vocabularies provides not just words that mean the same, but also many shades of meaning. We use the Anglo-Saxon or Old

English word 'read' in the same way as speakers of Latin languages use derivations of 'legere', from which we get 'legible'. Yet readable and legible mean different things. To say text is readable means it is easy and enjoyable to read. To say it is legible just means it can be read.

On top of those two sets of words are thousands of words we have adopted and continue to adopt from languages all over the world. These range from everyday words like 'pyjamas' (from Persian) to more technical terms like 'electronics' (from Greek). Many of the later additions to English have been adopted for specific purposes, often into specialized fields of knowledge, and may not be widely understood. You stand a better chance of being immediately understood if you choose words that have been in use for a long time.

### vi. Negative expressions

Avoiding negative expressions doesn't mean saying something is good when it's bad. It means expressing your ideas in a positive way. Ideas that are expressed positively are easier to understand as you can see here:

| Negative | Positive |
|---|---|
| does not have | lacks |
| does not include | leaves out |
| don't ignore | listen to |

| don't use | avoid |
|-----------|-------|
| not many | few |
| not often | rarely |
| not unless | only if |

If you say you are 'not proud' of something you have done, the listener has to conjure up two ideas in quick succession – what it means to be proud and that you were not whatever it is. If instead you say you 'regret' it, the listener has only one idea to grasp. Ideas that are expressed positively are also likely to be more definite than those expressed negatively. If you say 'I wasn't annoyed', it raises the question 'What did you feel?'. Saying one thing is 'not unlike' another requires the listener to do mental gymnastics and still leaves him or her with only a vague idea of what you mean.

When you are giving instructions, for example for filling in a form, it is particularly important to focus on what users should do rather than what they shouldn't. A string of negatives as in 'Do not press NO if you do not wish to continue' is liable to leave the user confused and uncertain. What is a user to make of an instruction such as 'If you do not wish to proceed without making any payment at all, click the Cancel button'? If you are aware that there may be problems in using your website, try to find a positive way of leading people through what they have to do. Instead of saying 'Don't proceed without installing X', say 'Before you go any further, you need to install X'.

### vii. Terms that date

When you are choosing words to use on a website, you need to think not only how they will read today, but whether they will make sense next week and next year. When you read an old newspaper or magazine, you are reading a self-contained document, every page of which has a date on it. When you look at a website it is not so simple. As a writer you want to rewrite as little as possible, so avoid terms like 'today' and 'last year' unless they are within a self-contained page or article that you can put a date on.

This could sometimes be a little hard on your reader. As readers, we find it easier to take in relative rather than absolute reference points. So 'tomorrow' is easier to take in than 'on Wednesday' because 'on Wednesday' requires us to think what day it is today before we can work out how far away Wednesday is. But this is one area where I recommend that a writer should be selfish and avoid unnecessary work by using absolute terms. You can still use relative terms in other areas. For example, 'he earns half as much as she does' is easier to take in than 'he earns £25,000 a year compared with her £50,000', which requires your readers to do the calculation themselves.

You also need to think how a word will be interpreted when the material around it has changed. For example, before the start of a football competition a sports commentator called Robinson may write a series of articles giving his opinion of each team. For these articles to be relevant throughout the competition, they need to be carefully labelled. If the link to the relevant article reads 'Robinson's verdict' that will be fine before the matches are played, but once the website starts reporting results, users would expect a link called 'Robinson's verdict' to lead to Robinson's verdict on the match, not his opinion of the teams before they started.

So far this chapter has been about what to avoid. That may itself seem negative, but 'avoid' is a positive way of saying 'don't use'. Besides, advice is often best understood by seeing what happens when you ignore it. We learn more from mistakes than successes, and rules are nearly always drawn up as a result of things going wrong. You may know a website called WebPagesThatSuck.com, which aims to help people learn how to design websites by showing them examples of bad design.

### How to make bad writing better

Now that we've looked at the kinds of words and phrases to avoid, let's see what more you can do to improve a really bad piece of writing. You can go through crossing out unnecessary words, you can replace phrases with single words and you can replace long words derived from Latin with shorter ones. But you can only go so far. You may still have a bad bit of prose. To rewrite it radically, you have to look at the structure of the language. Here's an example of a long-winded office memo:

> The position in regard to office accommodation at the present time is
> characterized by a shortfall of four hundred square metres in terms of

> the need versus availability. The space situation requires review on a monthly basis. An immediate solution is not a practicable proposition, but we have absolute confidence in the ability of the facilities department to maximize their efforts and it is envisaged that an overall solution will materialize in the short to medium term.

You can change 'at the present time' to 'now' and replace 'maximize their efforts' with 'try hard'. You know that 'short to medium term' is meaningless unless you have a timetable, so you can put 'soon' instead. But the problem is not just in the particular words chosen: it is in the kinds of words they are. To make it better, you need to read the piece through, work out what the writer is trying to say and express those ideas differently. It could go something like this:

> We need four hundred square metres more office space. We should review the position every month. There is no immediate solution, but we are sure the facilities department are doing their best and will come up with something soon.

What did I do? First I put in a personal pronoun, 'we'. This is a message from a manager to staff about something that affects them directly. It should be written in a personal way, from me to you, not impersonally as if it were a description of something happening elsewhere. Here are some more examples:

| Impersonal | Personal |
|---|---|
| A fault has become apparent. | I have made a mistake. |
| A preferential rate is not an option. | We cannot offer you a preferential rate. |
| It is not our wish to be impersonal. | We do not wish to seem impersonal. |
| Your disappointment is apparent. | You are obviously disappointed. |

### i. Change the construction

By starting the first sentence with 'We', you change the construction of the sentence. Instead of an impersonal, passive construction ('The position is characterized by a shortfall of ...'), you have a personal, active one ('We are ... short'). That allows you to get rid of the vague words and phrases like 'The position in regard to', 'is characterized by', 'a shortfall of' and 'in terms of the need versus availability'.

The same applies to the second sentence. By replacing a passive construction ('The space situation requires review') with an active one ('We need to review'), not only have you shortened it, you have included more information: you have said who needs to do the review. One reason the passive voice is used so often is that it is a way of avoiding responsibility. 'It is envisaged that a solution...' in the third sentence does just that. It appears to give the staff information, but unless they know who to go back to when the problem is not solved, it is useless.

The key to constructing sentences that work is to know what job the words in a sentence do, what their function is. When you are choosing words, you need to think not only of their meaning but how they will work together most efficiently. That's a roundabout way of saying it helps to understand the grammar. You have a choice of ways of conveying the same idea and the obvious choice here is whether to use nouns or verbs. The verbose version of the manager's message contains twenty nouns and seven verbs. The concise version contains eight nouns and six verbs.

### ii. Use more verbs and fewer nouns

The long-winded memo is hard to understand because the writer chose to use a lot of nouns to get the message across. What is more, the nouns are nearly all abstract ('position', 'regard', 'basis', etc). And the verbs in the long-winded version are weak ('is', 'have', etc) and nearly all in the passive. In the concise version, the proportion of verbs to nouns is higher and there are more pronouns – three rather than one – because it comes from people ('we') and talks about people ('we', 'they') rather than using abstract ideas like 'shortfall' and 'availability'.

Why do people write like that? Typically it happens when they represent organizations, rather than writing as individuals. Organizations are impersonal and focused on things like products, policies, structures and targets. Even when focused on people, they put them in categories like 'suppliers', 'voters', 'staff' or 'customers'. When you want to book a holiday, the airline will tell you they 'have availability'. When you complain about service, they'll say, 'Customer satisfaction is our highest priority.' Their focus is on things that can be measured. So when they write, they think first of nouns, often abstract ones, like 'availability', 'satisfaction' and 'priorities', and then think of ways of linking them together. It's a kind of knitting with nouns. It tends to get tangled and, yes, woolly, as you can see here:

| Abstract | Concrete |
|---|---|
| collateral damage | civilians being killed |
| downsizing | people losing their jobs |
| embedment of new structures | staff happy with their new jobs |
| good inter-personal skills | getting on with people |
| offer a convenient resource | help |
| sourcing content | finding words and pictures |

### iii. Be specific

Good, clear writing is like telling stories. Choosing verbs rather than nouns focuses your attention on action, on people doing things. Your aim is to transmit as clear a picture as you can to the other person, and you are more likely to succeed if you talk about specific people and things they can visualize. If someone tells you a boxer 'suffered brain damage', you get a picture of a person in a boxing ring or in hospital. That's already quite a strong picture, but if someone tells you instead that the boxer's 'brain was damaged', your mind's eye goes to his head, like a camera zooming in to the detail. A small change of words makes a dramatic difference.

If you need a reminder of what things like nouns, pronouns and verbs are, the next chapter should help. If you are confident about grammar, you can skip it.

## Checklist

- Avoid jargon, slang and any words and phrases that exclude people.
- If you use abbreviations, explain them at least once on every page.
- Avoid clichés because they are second-hand phrases.
- Prefer short words, usually of German origin, to long words of Latin origin.
- Express your ideas positively.
- Think how your words will read tomorrow or next year.
- Choose verbs rather than nouns to convey your ideas.
- Talk about real people and things.

# The functions of words

Here we go into the jobs that words do. This brief review of grammar explains the main parts of speech – nouns, pronouns, verbs, adjectives and adverbs.

## Parts of speech

We are now looking at the jobs that words do – their grammatical function, as opposed to their meaning. The word 'fast', for example, has different functions in 'I fast once a year' and 'He ends his fast when the sun sets.' In the first sentence it is a verb, expressing action, and in the second it is a noun, a thing.

Some jokes work by playing with the function of words. A notorious wartime newspaper headline read 'French push bottles up German rear'. The writer intended 'push' to be a noun meaning 'advance', but if 'push' is a verb it reads very differently.

In the previous chapter we looked at a piece of bad writing, worked out what it was trying to say, and then tried to express the same ideas more clearly. We ended up with far fewer nouns in proportion to verbs. One way of improving a piece of poor writing is to look at each noun and see if you can convey the same meaning using a verb instead.

For example, you might be asked in a letter to 'supply the date of inheritance with regard to your holding of x'. As soon as you see 'with regard to', you can sense that you are in the presence of a long-winded writer. The writer was forced to use it after choosing to use a noun 'inheritance' rather than the verb 'to inherit'. Having chosen a noun, the only way of linking the idea of inheriting to what was inherited was with the phrase 'with regard to'. Had the writer chosen the verb instead, it would have been possible to write 'the date you inherited your holding of x'. With the verb you go straight from the idea of inheriting to what was inherited. You don't need a woolly phrase to link them. You use fewer words to say the same thing and your meaning is clearer.

A simple analogy for the main parts of speech is a human body. The nouns are the bones. As the skeleton defines the shape and identity of the body, so the nouns are the things we write about, the subject matter, the hard bits. The verbs are the muscles, the bits that act, the dynamic part. The adjectives and adverbs are the fat. They are, as their names suggest, the add-on words. Adjectives add meaning to nouns and adverbs add meaning to verbs. A little fat is pleasing to the eye and the touch. Fat adds flavour to food and makes us feel good, but a lot of fat makes us flabby and unhealthy. The analogy is not perfect, but you can see where it leads: effective writing is muscular and dynamic, with just enough fat to give it a bit of flavour.

So be guided by these three rules:
1. Concentrate on the verbs. They are the key element in a sentence. They express action or a state of being.
2. Choose nouns that enable you to talk about real people and things wherever possible.
3. Be sparing with adjectives and adverbs. If you've chosen your nouns and verbs well, you shouldn't need many add-ons.

If you think of writing as a craft and words as your tools, you need to know them as well as you can. You need to be able to play with them, to try them in different combinations and orders. This means understanding what words mean and how they function grammatically. We all have an idea of how our language works. We absorb it and practise it from our earliest childhood. But if you are sure what function each word performs in a sentence, your writing will be much better than if you have only a rough idea.

This table shows how we can express the same ideas in different ways using different parts of speech:

| Noun | Verb | Adjective | Adverb |
|------|------|-----------|--------|
| rebel | rebel (pronounced re-*bel*) | rebellious | rebelliously |
| speech | speak | spoken | (orally) |
| success | succeed | successful | successfully |
| use | use (pronounced *yooz*) | useful | usefully |

We don't always have a complete set of words, because language develops randomly according to how it is used, rather than as the result of a systematic plan. Note, for example, that for an adverb expressing the idea of speaking we use 'orally', not 'spokenly'.

Test yourself. In the following sentence, identify one verb, four nouns and two adjectives:

> The design provides a fisheye view of three levels of content.

The verb, expressing the action or state of being we are talking about, is 'provides'. The four nouns are 'design', 'view', 'levels' and 'content'. The two adjectives are 'fisheye' and 'three'. Each adds meaning to one of the nouns in the sentence. What kind of 'view' do you get? It's a wider view than you get with a human eye without moving it. ('Fisheye' in this case is a noun being used as an adjective.) How many levels can you see? Three.

In this next sentence, there are two verbs, three nouns, two adjectives and one adverb:

> A good website loads quickly and gives the user relevant information.

The verbs are 'loads' and 'gives'. The three nouns are 'website', 'user' and 'information'. The adjectives are 'good' and 'relevant'. The adverb, which adds meaning to the verb 'loads', is 'quickly'. In another sentence, 'loads' might have a different function. For example, in 'This website contains loads of information', 'loads' is a noun and the verb is 'contains'.

One part of speech we have mentioned but not defined is the pronoun. As its name suggests, a pronoun stands in place of a noun. Using a pronoun instead of a noun makes sentences flow by avoiding irritating repetition. So instead of saying 'Jo boasted that Jo had a website that brought Jo a lot of business', we say 'Jo boasted that he had a website that brought him a lot of business'. After we have established who we are talking about, replacing 'Jo' with two pronouns, 'he' and 'him', makes the sentence flow.

We'll now go through the main parts of speech one by one to help you make your writing as sharp as possible.

### Nouns

Nouns (often indicated in dictionaries by the abbreviation *n*) are the names of people or things. They answer the question 'Who?' or 'What?'. They are either concrete or abstract. A person is concrete, in the sense of being real; and concrete things are animal, vegetable or mineral. Abstract nouns are ideas, concepts, things you can't touch. By abstracting your thoughts from real people and things, you are able to develop theories that you can then apply to all relevant situations, rather than starting from scratch every time. Abstract nouns are for talking about principles and theories. They should be kept in their place.

In much of life, abstract nouns tend to get in the way of understanding. They may even be used deliberately to distort the truth or to hide the fact that the writer has nothing to say. Usually they just create a fog. Think how much clearer the word 'documents' is than 'documentation'. Why say 'Our preference would be for greater consistency in the appearance of the logo', using three abstract nouns? It would be clearer if you said 'We want the same logo on every page.' When stating the aim of your site, you may be tempted to get a bit philosophical and talk about 'enhancement' of this or that. It is more effective to describe what you are offering in concrete terms. Writing on websites for the most part should deal in real things that people can visualize and quantify.

Nouns are singular or plural. You are either talking about one person or thing, or several. It's obvious, but it's amazing how many sentences start by talking about one thing and end up talking about several, and vice versa, thus confusing the reader. Collective nouns are groups of things or people, such as the staff of a company. They usually count as a single noun. Again it's easy to find examples of writing where collective nouns start singular (as in 'The staff is recruited from the surrounding area') and end up plural (as in 'The staff frequently contribute to the website'). It's not a dreadful mistake; the meaning will be understood. But consciously or unconsciously the reader will be aware of an inconsistency. It shows the writer has not thought carefully enough about the ideas he or she wants to convey.

## Pronouns

Pronouns stand in for nouns. Like nouns they answer the question 'Who?' or 'What?'. Pronouns (often indicated in dictionaries by the abbreviation *pron*) are useful devices for referring to someone or something the second time you mention them. They help the flow of the writing by providing a kind of shorthand. Instead of repeating a title and a name – for example, 'the Chief Executive, Mary Jones' – you just say 'she' the second time you mention her and the reader will know who you mean. The problems arise when you have been talking about her so long that the reader can't remember who she is. Two or three times is probably as much as a reader can cope with. And if you are talking about more than one person or thing, you need to be careful to avoid confusion.

On a website, we mostly want to use the pronouns 'I', 'we' and 'you'. By starting sentences with these words, we establish a sense of dialogue between the website producer and the user.

### Adjectives

Adjectives (often indicated in dictionaries by the abbreviation *adj*) describe people or things. They answer the question 'What is it (or he or she) like?' They add meaning to nouns and pronouns. My advice is to be sparing with adjectives. Using a lot of them can be counterproductive. Instead of adding meaning to your nouns, they may dilute their meaning or confuse the reader. Take the example of 'a usual habit'. Adding 'usual' does not give extra weight to the idea you are trying to convey – a habit is by definition something usual. On the contrary, the adjective draws attention away from the noun and raises the possibility in the reader's mind that this habit may not be usual.

Using a lot of adjectives tends to draw attention to the descriptions rather than the things or people you are talking about. It's a kind of word-inflation and, as with real inflation, its effect is to devalue the currency. Calling things 'amazing', 'spectacular' or 'cool' is fine in conversation with friends, because we don't mean those words to be taken literally. All they tell our friends is that we like something. They are expressions of feeling, not fact. When you write, and especially when you write for people you don't know, your feelings are rarely relevant. You want to make your meaning clear and you need to use a stable currency.

## Verbs

Verbs (often indicated in dictionaries by the abbreviation *v* or *vb*) express doing or being. Without a verb, there is little or no meaning in a statement. In fact, if it hasn't got a verb in it we wouldn't call it a statement at all. Take political slogans. A few years after winning a huge majority in the general election of 1997, the Labour government was suddenly unpopular. The Prime Minister could no longer assume he had a huge lead in the opinion polls. The words that had seemed so powerful a short time before no longer carried weight. One political commentator remarked that Tony Blair was having to use verbs again: he was having to put meaning into his words. Slogans such as 'education, education, education' don't tell you much. They don't answer the question 'What are you doing about it?'

Verbs answer the question 'What?' in the sense of 'What happened?', 'What did she do?' or 'What about it?'. If you walk into a room and exclaim, 'My God, the cat!', the inevitable response will be, 'What about the cat?'. You have to say what you've done to it or what it has done, otherwise your exclamation does not mean much. You need to use a verb.

Whenever possible, use the active rather than the passive voice of the verb. In the sentence 'Our company makes widgets', the verb 'makes' is in the active voice. There is an action and you know who is doing it. The same idea could be expressed in the passive voice as 'Widgets are made' and you would not know who by, unless the writer adds 'by our company'. The passive voice tells the story from the point of view of the person or thing to whom the action is done, as you can see from this table:

| Passive | Active |
|---|---|
| Mistakes were found in the design. | Warren found mistakes in the design. |
| Steps have been taken to put it right. | I have taken steps to put it right. |
| The designer has been sacked. | Elaine has sacked the designer. |
| Warren and I will be given a bonus. | Elaine will give Warren and me a bonus. |

Suppose you are involved in an incident in the street. If you say 'I was hit', you are using the passive. You have told us something and we have an idea of what happened to you, but you have missed out a vital piece of information: who or what did it. If you add that information in the passive voice it will be 'I was hit by the blue car'. Using the active voice, you can say the same thing using fewer words, 'The blue car hit me'. Because of the way verbs are constructed in English, the active voice tends to use fewer words to say the same thing. Just as important when you can use only a certain number of words in a particular space on a Web page, the active voice says more in the same number of words than the passive. Suppose it was a person, not a car, that hit you. In three words, the passive

'I was hit' says only what happened to you. The active 'He hit me' says who did it as well.

If you want to tell a story from a particular person's point of view, then you may be right to use the passive, but in many cases the passive is a sign of lazy writing. It suggests that the writer wants to do only half the work needed. Worse, it can be used deliberately to avoid commitment or evade responsibility. 'Every effort will be made to solve your problem' is not as reassuring as 'I will make every effort to …' and 'An error was made in calculating your bill' leaves you fuming. Why can't they be honest and say 'We made an error'?

When you choose your verbs, remember the earlier advice to use a single word rather than a phrase whenever possible. Why say something 'was coincidental' when you have a perfectly good word 'coincided'? Why 'stage an inquiry into' when you can simply 'investigate', and so on? The phrase is weaker than the single word.

Verbs have tenses – different forms used to distinguish between the past, the present and the future. Your tenses should be consistent, so that the reader has a clear sense of the time of the actions you describe. 'He went to the site I had been working on' means he went there some time in the past and the 'I had' suggests that you are no longer working on the site. By contrast, 'He went to the site I have been working on' suggests you still are.

Agreement of tenses is especially important when reporting people's words. If you use the tenses correctly the reader knows exactly what was said. 'He said he would redesign the site' means what he said was 'I will redesign the site'. If someone says 'I may do it' those words are in the present tense. If you report his words to someone else, his statement is in the past – he said it – so his words are moved one tense into the past: 'He said he might do it.'

## Subject, verb and object

The verb has a subject – the doer or the person you are talking about. In this sense the word 'subject' is a specialized grammatical term and does not signify 'the thing the sentence is about'. Its grammatical meaning is quite precise: one word or phrase in a sentence is the subject of the verb. That word or phrase is a noun or pronoun, the person or thing performing the action. Take the verb 'to design'. If you say 'I design', 'design' is the verb and 'I' is the subject. Verbs often have objects, the thing or person the action is done to, to put it crudely. So in 'I design websites', 'I' is the subject, 'design' is the verb and the object is 'websites'.

This is the heart of the business of writing. If you can identify the building blocks – subject, verb, object – you can build anything you want. We 'construct' sentences (and 'build' websites). Writing is a craft that you can learn and practise. Choosing the right words is like choosing the right materials for whatever you are making. Constructing sentences is like putting the materials together so that the building, cricket bat or chair looks right and does what it is supposed to do. To use another metaphor, understanding language is like understanding a piece of machinery by looking at it carefully, or even taking it to pieces, to see how it works. You wouldn't say that knowing how to mend a puncture took the fun out of riding a bicycle; on the contrary, it should give you confidence.

There's one more point to make about verbs: subject and verb must agree. This is easy in English compared with languages such as French or Russian. There's really only one question to ask: Is the subject singular or plural? Most verbs in English don't change much when you change the subject, grammatically speaking. They go 'I design', 'you design' and so on. The only one that is different is the third person singular 'he designs' or 'she designs'. If the subject is singular, 'the Web' for example, you must use the singular verb, 'is', whereas if the subject is plural, 'the Web pages' for example, the verb must be 'are'.

One reason we get it wrong is that, unlike the French or the Russians, we don't have to think much about subject-verb agreement, so we often don't think at all. Another reason is that if we make our sentences long and complicated, by the time we get to the verb we have forgotten what the subject was. For example, 'The project leader, whose views were decisive in the design of the pages, now that they are up and customers are buying more widgets, have decided to move on.' Putting a lot of information between the subject and verb is what causes the confusion, especially if, as in this case, the subject is singular and the noun just before the verb is plural.

Here are some more examples of where subject–verb agreement can be tricky:

| Wrong | Right |
|---|---|
| A selection of laptops are available. | A selection of laptops is available. |
| It is you who is to blame. | It is you who are to blame. |
| Neither the colour nor the font are suitable. | Neither the colour nor the font is suitable. |
| There's many things I could tell you. | There are many things I could tell you. |

## Adverbs

After verbs come adverbs (often indicated in dictionaries by the abbreviation *adv*). They answer the question 'How?'. They are usually easy to recognize because most of them end in '-ly'. They describe actions. In grammatical terms, they 'qualify' or 'modify' verbs. They add meaning to verbs in the same way as adjectives add meaning to nouns. As with adjectives, my advice is to be sparing. Don't devalue the currency.

If you find yourself using a lot of adverbs, you are probably choosing weak verbs and using add-on words. The sentence 'This website works badly' uses a verb 'works' and an adverb 'badly'. The meaning is in the adverb, not the verb. A better sentence might be 'This website disappoints' or 'This website fails'. Here the meaning is in the verb and the sentence is shorter and clearer.

## Rules of grammar

This chapter has given you a brief look at the main functions of words, the jobs they do. The rules are there to help make your writing effective. If you are sure something you are writing would be more effective if you broke a rule, then break it. There is a world of difference between breaking a rule of grammar for a good reason and using language ineffectively because you don't understand how it works. It is more important to keep in mind what you are trying to achieve than to remember all the rules. You can always look them up.

## Checklist

- As well as knowing what words mean, you need to know their grammatical function.
- The main parts of speech are verbs, nouns, pronouns, adjectives and adverbs.
- The verb is the key element in a sentence, expressing action or a state of being.
- Nouns are people or things. Choose concrete rather than abstract nouns.
- Pronouns replace nouns to avoid repetition.
- Adjectives and adverbs are add-ons, to be used sparingly.
- Nouns and pronouns are the subjects of verbs. Subject and verb must agree.
- The active voice of the verb is shorter and more informative than the passive.
- Rules of grammar are there to help make your writing effective.
- If you break them, do it for a good reason.

# Constructing sentences

> Having taken the language to pieces, we now look at how to build the parts of speech into phrases, clauses and sentences. This chapter explains the importance of putting words in the right order and gives you advice on how to improve your sentences.

Choose the right words and put them in the right order. That's the advice for writing well. I've given you some rules for choosing words – words that accurately convey your meaning, single words rather than phrases, no jargon, no clichés, simple familiar words rather than long pompous ones, and so on. We've broken the language down into its individual parts and defined their functions. Now we're dealing with how to put them together.

## The right order

The order of words is more important in English than in many other languages. We had a hint of the difference between English and most other European languages when we were dealing with subject–verb agreement on page 93. In general, English words do not change their endings as they change their relationship with other words. You do not have to learn long lists of verbs and their endings, or nouns and theirs. For the most part, the only verb-ending that differs from the others is the third person singular which has an 's' on the end. We say 'he writes' or 'she writes', but for 'I', 'you', 'we' and 'they' the ending is the same – 'I write', 'you write', 'we write' and 'they write'. In French, almost all of those endings would be different. English nouns don't change endings at all. We don't change the ending of the word 'Moscow' according to whether we are going there or are there already. In Russian, we would have to.

The changing endings (inflections) that existed in Old English, mostly disappeared nearly a thousand years ago, as did the classification of nouns into masculine, feminine and neuter. The change made English grammar simpler and English a more flexible language. But it also made the order of words important. In Latin, you can write the words of a sentence in almost any order and the overall meaning is still clear because each word contains in itself its relationship to the other words. But you have to use the correct form of each word to express your meaning. In English, however, 'Joe shot Peter' means one thing and 'Peter shot Joe' means something quite different. The meaning is dictated not by the form of the words themselves, but by the order you put them in.

While we're on the subject of inflections, as with all rules there are exceptions. English does retain a few words that change and they do cause problems. If we had used a pronoun in the example in the previous paragraph, we could not have changed the meaning just by changing the order. 'He shot Peter' could not be turned round to 'Peter shot he'; we would have to say 'Peter shot him'. Pronouns are some of the very few words left that do change according to their relationship to other words in the sentence. 'I' is 'I' when it is the subject and 'me' when it is the object. 'You' stays the same. 'He' changes to 'him', 'she' changes to 'her', 'we' to 'us' and 'they' to 'them'.

The relative pronoun 'who', which becomes 'whom' when it is the object, is one that causes problems. On page 13, I said that the second of the three questions you should ask yourself before you start writing is 'For whom?'. That is correct, though it does sound a bit pompous. Perhaps that's why some people think they are showing off their erudition by using 'whom'. Unfortunately they often get it wrong.

It is correct to say 'I saw the man whom I commissioned to set up the database.' The noun 'man' is the object of the verb 'saw' and the pronoun that you use for him in the subordinate clause is the object of the verb 'commissioned'. (Most of us would leave the relative pronoun out anyway and just say '… the man I commissioned…') It is not correct to say 'I saw the man whom I thought was setting up the database.' because in this sentence the emphasis has shifted. Whereas 'commissioned' has an object, 'thought' does not. You wouldn't say 'I thought him was setting up the database'; you would use 'he'. The man is now the subject of the verb 'was setting up', so the relative pronoun should be 'who'.

We got into inflections, or the lack of them, in order to point out the importance of getting words in the right order. As a rule you should put words next to, or as close as possible to, the words to which they relate most closely. Otherwise your meaning may be ambiguous.

The ambiguity may be serious, as in 'The judge ruled that statements made about the attack in court should not be broadcast', which leaves you not knowing whether it was the attack or the statements that were made in court. It may be comic, as in 'I know a man with a wooden leg called Mick', to which the reply comes 'Really? What's his other leg called?' Sometimes the clumsy ordering just makes a sentence hard to follow, as in these instructions for setting up a computer: 'Make sure correct voltage shows in voltage switch window for your location.' This would be better as, 'Make sure correct voltage for your location shows in voltage switch window.'

If you get into a tangle trying to get the right words next to each other, you are probably trying to pack too much information into one sentence. Break up the information into two or more sentences. My advice is to keep your sentences short. Writing short sentences forces you to think about what you are saying and makes it easier for the reader. It's not that you can't write good long sentences. It's just that the longer your sentences are, the greater the chance that something will go wrong.

## Sentences, phrases and clauses

What is a sentence? A sentence expresses a complete idea. In grammatical terms, it needs to contain a finite verb, that is a verb with a subject. A phrase need not. A phrase is a group of words that functions as a single word. 'The background colour of my site' is a phrase. The words are in a certain order, so the phrase has meaning, but if you walked into a room and said it, it wouldn't make sense on its own. People would be waiting for more information. If you said 'The background colour of my site is yellow', the phrase would function as a noun and be the subject of the verb 'is' and you would have made a sentence.

A phrase may contain a verb or part of a verb. In 'having designed the site map', 'having designed' is a verb, or rather part of a verb, but the phrase does not make sense on its own. 'Having' is a participle; it cannot be the only verb in a sentence. You are waiting for the sentence to be completed, perhaps like this: 'Having designed the site map, Sarah started thinking about the contacts page.' 'Having designed the site map' is a phrase which functions as a single word describing the activities of Sarah, who is the subject of the verb 'started'.

A clause does contain a finite verb. It may make sense on its own or not. It depends how you use it. 'Although he improved the navigation on the site' is a clause. It contains the verb 'improved', whose subject is 'he', but it does not make sense on its own. The first word 'although' tells you that you are waiting for more information. So it is called a 'subordinate' or 'dependent' clause: it depends on another clause to complete the idea. 'Although he improved the navigation on the site, he continued to get complaints' is a sentence. The clause we added, 'he continued to get complaints', is the main clause of the sentence. A main clause makes sense on its own.

A common fault in writing is using what's called a hanging participle, clause or phrase. A famous example is 'After the Queen had named the ship, she slid gracefully into the water.' It happens when you write a descriptive clause or phrase and don't follow it with the person it applies to, as in 'Having designed the site map, the client told Sarah she didn't like it.' Grammatically, this means the client designed the site map. The intended meaning may become clear from the context, but there is an ambiguity there and you are expecting the reader to work out what you mean. You, the writer, should find another way of saying it, such as 'The client said she didn't like the site map Sarah had designed' or 'After all the work Sarah had put in to the site map, the client said she didn't like it.'

Starting every sentence with the subject can get monotonous. You will want to vary the rhythm of your writing by starting some sentences with a descriptive clause or phrase. But make sure you follow it with whatever is being described so that your meaning is unambiguous.

A sentence consisting of one clause, a main clause, is called a simple sentence. A sentence with two or more equal clauses, usually joined together by 'and' or 'but', is called a compound sentence. A sentence with a main clause and one or more subordinate clauses is called a complex sentence. Those are technical terms, but the distinction they make fits well with the general advice of the *Desktop Guide*: keep your writing simple. Compound and complex sentences require the reader to keep several bits of information in mind at once. The longer and more complicated a sentence is, the greater the chance that the reader will lose the thread or misunderstand the information. On your home page and the pages immediately below it in the hierarchy of your site, where your text is sparse and the user is scanning for information, simple sentences are almost a must. Further down the hierarchy, where your text is denser and users are into something they have chosen to read, you can and should vary the rhythm of your writing with a mixture of simple, compound and complex sentences.

## Writing good sentences

There are a few other tips for writing good sentences. The first is to keep the same subject throughout a sentence. That makes it easier to follow. A simple sentence has only one clause and therefore only one subject. The problem comes when you put several ideas into one sentence. Changing subject in the middle of a sentence forces the reader to make an extra mental effort to follow your train of thought, as these examples show:

| Changing subject | Same subject |
|---|---|
| As *I* know very little about websites, *you* would be the best person to design my new site. | As *I* know very little about websites, *I*'d like you to design my new site. |
| The *pilot site* had a generally favourable reaction from users, but negative *opinions* were expressed about the search facility. | *Users* generally reacted favourably to the pilot site, but were not impressed with the search facility. |
| *Interviews* have now taken place and all the *bids* have been scrutinized and *we* have decided to give the website contract to you. | *We* have interviewed the applicants and scrutinized all the bids and *we* have decided to give the website contract to you. |

Another way of making your sentences flow is to express the ideas in them in a similar way. That often means using the same part of speech – verbs, nouns or adjectives. The sentence 'I opposed the project because of the cost and the manager disliked me' uses a noun to express one objection (the cost), and a verb to express the other (the manager disliked me). It doesn't flow well. It would be better to say either '...because it was going to cost millions and the manager disliked me' or '...because of the cost and the fact that the manager disliked me'. Then the ideas are balanced and easier to follow.

The third thing to think about in your sentences is where to place the important words. Just as supermarkets have developed a science of placing goods where they are most likely to be bought, so writers should place words where they will have the greatest impact. The prime spots in a sentence are the beginning and the end. If you get into the habit of reading your work out loud, you will be aware of the rhythm of your sentences and the importance of ending on a strong word or phrase, rather than tailing off on a weak one.

On a website, where your text is likely to be shorter and more broken up than in print, the first and last words of your sentences are more exposed. When users scan a page, they tend to read only the first word or two of a line, so make sure the first sentence in every paragraph starts with a strong word or phrase.

## Checklist

- Put your words in the right order: as close as possible to the words they relate to.
- If you find it hard to put the right words together, break up your sentence.
- A sentence expresses a complete idea. It must contain a verb.
- A sentence with one clause is a simple sentence.
- A sentence with more than one clause is a compound or complex sentence.
- Keep your sentences short.
- Don't use a lot of subordinate clauses.
- Keep the same subject throughout a sentence.
- Try to make sentences flow by expressing ideas in a similar way.
- Place important words at the beginning and the end.

# Spelling

Here we look briefly at spelling and style because of the need to be consistent and look professional.

### Spelling old and new

'Commynycacyon.' That's how William Caxton spelt 'communication' more than five hundred years ago. When he set up the first printing press in England, Caxton had to decide which of many versions of English spelling to use. Some of his decisions are with us today, though 'commynycacyon' is not one of them. It took several hundred years for English spelling to be standardized. Even in the twentieth century it was still changing. A standard reference book published in 1911 preferred 'inflexion' and 'Shakspere' to the current 'inflection' and 'Shakespeare'.

The idea, however, of having to work out what individual writers mean by their own ways of spelling is long gone. We expect to be able to recognize words immediately, especially now that communication is so fast. Just as the layout, navigation, links and other features of websites have quickly become standardized, so the language used on a site should be standardized in order to be instantly recognizable.

We don't expect everyone to spell every word exactly the same way. Many words are spelt differently in American and British English, so what is a mistake in one may not be in the other. But within each system there are correct and incorrect spellings and a website is undermined by mistakes or inconsistencies. Users don't necessarily notice every mistake, but consciously or unconsciously they register an inconsistency which undermines their confidence in the site.

Beware the computer spellchecker. It may draw your attention to mistakes and encourage you to reread your text, but you can't rely on it. Volumes could be written about the mess it gets you into, quite apart from the laziness it induces. It inspired this poem I read in an in-flight magazine:

> I have a spelling checker. It came with my PC.
> It plainly marks four my revue mistakes I cannot sea.
> I've run this poem threw it. I'm sure your please to no
> Its letter perfect in it's weigh. My checker tolled me sew.

Far better to rely on your own editorial eye and to keep a dictionary beside you.

For the most part, you can rely on a dictionary, but on recent additions to the language you may have to decide for yourself. You've probably noticed that there is as yet no agreed spelling of some of the words we use on websites. Should it be 'website' or 'Web site'? How do you spell 'online'? Some people write 'on-line'. Sometimes it is 'on line'. And the companies that work on the Web are described in a variety of ways – 'dot com', 'dot-com', 'dotcom' or even 'dot.com'.

## The Desktop Guide's style

In this *Desktop Guide*, I start 'Web' with a capital letter because it is a proper noun: there is only one Web. I write 'Web pages' to distinguish them from printed pages, but 'websites' because there are no other sites to confuse them with: websites have become a distinct class of thing. I write 'online', both for the adjective in 'online shopping' and for where you are when you use a website. Although it might be more logical to write 'I am on line', the meaning is not as obvious as it is in 'I am online'. When you say it, you will probably put the stress on the second syllable, 'line', whereas in the adjective you would put it on the first syllable, 'on'.

I favour 'dotcom'. It combines the word 'dot' with an abbreviation of another word 'com'. The two parts need to be tied together to form an adjective and it doesn't seem to fit the usual argument for a hyphen. What about 'email'? It is more difficult as it is a combination of a single letter with a word. Quite a lot of people write 'e-mail'. Should we write 'e-commerce' or 'ecommerce'? I put 'email' all in one, but hyphenate 'e-commerce'. My reason is that, while 'email' may not be universal, it is the most common spelling among Web users and it is not likely to be misread; whereas 'ecommerce' starts the same way as a lot of other words, such as 'economic' and 'ecology', and could be misread.

Because this book is part of a series of Desktop Guides, I also take account of the publisher's house style. Because the book is published in Britain, it uses British rather than American spellings, although the publisher prefers a 'z' to an 's' in words like 'organize' and 'realize'.

Just as I had to decide on a style for this book and stick to it, so you must decide on a style for your website and make sure you spell words consistently throughout the site. Consistency is even more important in a website than in a book because users can go from page to page in almost any order.

**Checklist**

- Mistakes in spelling make your website less credible.
- It's best to check your own text, rather than relying on a spellchecker.
- Decide what spelling you will use and use it consistently.

# Punctuation

This chapter contains definitions of the punctuation marks you will need to make your writing clear and advice on how to use them.

Punctuation helps the reader by showing the structure of your sentences and removing any ambiguity. You have chosen the best words you can and put them in the right order. The punctuation is the finishing touch. Just to show what punctuation can do, take these words and see what they mean to you:

woman without her man is an empty vessel

Without punctuation, it looks like one sentence with 'woman' as the subject, so it means that a woman is incomplete without a man. With punctuation, you can reverse the meaning:

Woman! Without her, man is an empty vessel.

Punctuation is a powerful tool. Some legal documents are deliberately written without commas because the difference that a comma can make to an inheritance or a dispute is so great that some lawyers think it is safer to do without them than to risk putting one in the wrong place. There is an argument for using as little punctuation as possible on websites, but it has to do with the visual impression rather than legal arguments. Think of punctuation as marks added to your text and you can see why a lot of punctuation marks can make a Web page look messy.

### Capital letters

The standard uses of capital letters are at the beginning of a sentence and at the beginning of names of particular people and things. So this sentence starts with a capital 'S' and the *Desktop Guide* has capital 'D' and 'G' because it is the name of this particular book and references to it should stand out in the text. The point of capital letters is to draw the reader's eye to the start of something important. Capitals should be used sparingly, otherwise the eye gets confused.

Avoid writing text all in capital letters; a title perhaps, and some headings, but no sentences or long bits of text, as in Figure 9. We are used to recognizing the shapes of words and sentences rather than reading every letter. We find it hard to read words written entirely in capitals because capitals have fewer distinctive features than lower-case letters. We are used to reading text that is mostly in lower case with a few capitals as highlights.

We recognize words by their shape,
especially by the bits at the top
rather than the bits at the bottom.

**CAPITAL LETTERS HAVE NO BITS ABOVE
OR BELOW, SO WORDS IN CAPITALS ARE
HARD TO RECOGNIZE.**

The irony is that when writers put important information in capitals precisely to draw our attention to it, we tend to skip it.

On a website, you need to be particularly careful about starting too many words with a capital. Your text is scattered, you tend to have more headings and titles than you do in printed text and you have navigation which in effect consists of headings because every link leads to a new page or section of a page.

The convention in print and on some websites is that every word in a heading or title should start with a capital letter. This is all right when a heading is three words long. Once you have more than three words, a heading begins to lose its impact and becomes harder to read if every word starts with a capital. One thing you can do is not to use a capital on the minor words like 'and', 'or' and 'with', but even so, the capital letters tend to interrupt the flow of the words. If you followed the print convention, you might have a home page where almost every word started with a capital letter. My advice is to put a capital on only the first word of a heading or link.

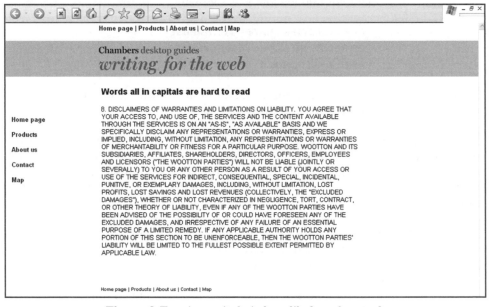

**Figure 9** Text in capitals is less likely to be read.

## Bold and other devices

If it's a good idea to use capitals sparingly, the same goes for other devices that draw attention: changes of font or colour, different sizes of font, italics, underlining and bold or highlighting. On a website, underlining is out because it might be confused with a link, and italics do not show up well on a screen. For the rest, remember that the function of these devices is to create contrast. If you emphasize everything, you emphasize nothing and if you use too many different devices, the user ends up confused, as is likely to be the case in Figure 10.

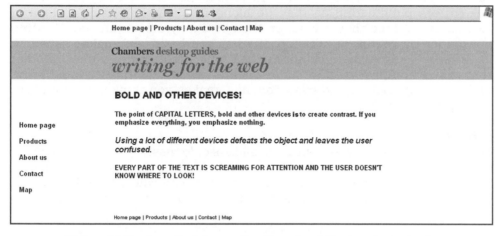

**Figure 10** Devices that draw attention should be used sparingly.

### Full stops and other endings

We mark the end of a sentence with a full stop, an exclamation mark or a question mark. Like capitals, exclamation marks and question marks are emphatic marks and should be used sparingly. Exclamation marks can suggest that writers are showing off or are not sure their words will be taken the right way. A lot of exclamations and questions on a screen can be tiresome.

Don't be afraid of full stops, however. With some text, you feel you can see the writers punctuating as they go along and simply putting a dash or comma every time they pause, as though they were frightened of losing the reader by putting a full stop. If what you have said makes sense on its own, if it expresses a complete idea, put a full stop and start another sentence. Forcing yourself to write in sentences is a good discipline. Trying to do without dashes, and even commas, makes you think carefully about what you are writing.

### Ellipsis

Three dots together are known as an ellipsis or 'omission marks'. They show that words have been left out. If you are quoting someone, using the ellipsis allows you to use the best parts of what he or she said, at the length you want. It has the advantage of suggesting that you are taking the trouble to quote accurately.

The ellipsis has also come to mean 'and so on'. Microsoft, for example, uses it in menus. In some versions of Microsoft Word®, if an item in a menu is followed by an ellipsis you soon learn that if you click on it you will be offered more options. In other versions, menus show a few items followed by '...' and users know that if they hold on, a longer list will come up. It has become common on websites to use this mark to tell the user that there is more to come. The ellipsis is meant to entice you by keeping a visual thread of communication going. However, while it does entice, it would be better if the words did the job on their own. It's as if the writer does not have confidence in the words he or she has chosen. At its worst, the ellipsis gives the impression that the writer can't be bothered to finish the sentence and is in effect saying, 'You know the rest.'

## Commas

The comma, as lawyers have found, can cause problems. There are no hard rules for when to use a comma. Some people see them as important to show the grammatical structure of a sentence by marking off subordinate clauses from the main clause. Others prefer to see them as natural pauses in the sense of the words, to help the text 'breathe'. My advice is to use commas sparingly. If most of your sentences are short and crisp, you shouldn't need many commas. It's a good idea to choose your words first, then put in commas where they are needed – to show the structure, mark pauses or eliminate ambiguity. The commas should help the sense of the words and not hinder the flow.

Commas replace 'and' in lists. Rather than write 'design and colour and text', we write 'design, colour and text'. In a list of single words you should not need a comma before 'and', but in a longer, more complicated list you may add one to make the meaning clear. Even in a simple list, you may use a comma to emphasize the last item, as in 'He was rude, untidy, and inefficient.' If your descriptive words are not a list, you don't need a comma. For example, in 'an untidy young man' the two adjectives progressively describe the man more precisely, with the more general 'young' next to the noun. It would be wrong to separate them with a comma as though you might have used 'and' instead. You would not say 'He is an untidy and young man.'

Use commas in pairs to mark words that add information that is not essential to the sentence. You should put a pair of commas round a short description, as in 'John Smith, the famous actor, is appearing this week at the Magnifico Theatre.' The phrase 'the famous actor' adds information, but is not essential. In the sentence 'The comma, as lawyers have found, can cause problems', the commas are round the subordinate clause. Without the words between the commas, you have a simple sentence 'The comma can cause problems.' On the other hand, don't make the mistake of putting commas round words that are necessary to the meaning of the sentence, as in 'Actors, who forget their lines, are always booed by the audience.' And don't confuse the reader by forgetting the second comma in a pair, as in 'The World Wide Web, which was invented by Tim Berners-Lee has grown at an astonishing rate.'

Commas are also used in figures to help make large numbers recognizable. Different countries have different conventions about where to place the comma, which may be why you see so many large numbers now written without them. Or could it just be laziness? To me, there's no doubt that '40,000' is easier to take in than '40000'.

## Parentheses

You can use brackets and pairs of dashes in the same way as pairs of commas. It's called putting words or information in parenthesis. You can also use brackets to mark off a whole sentence as not essential, but it's not a good idea to use a lot of brackets as it suggests that you are not sure whether the information should be in or out. On the other hand, brackets are useful for providing technical information, such as an equivalent measurement, as in 'It cost $600 (£340)', or a scientific name, as in 'salt (sodium chloride)'.

## Semicolons

The semicolon marks a slightly longer pause than a comma, but if you write short sentences you will not often need it. It is used to tie two contrasting ideas together as I did on page 42 when I wrote 'If you use these words, you're in; if you use those words, you're out.' Each idea could have stood as a separate sentence but the contrast is stronger when they are tied together.

The most common use of the semicolon is to separate listed items when you have a list within the list. Having semicolons marking the items in the main list allows you to use commas for the smaller list without confusion, as in 'The *Desktop Guide* helps you with all aspects of writing for the Web: the peculiarities of the Web; the purpose of your website; who it's for and what it's about; and the mechanics of writing, including grammar, spelling and punctuation.'

You may want to use a list like that in the body of some text, but if the list is an important one, high up the hierarchy of your site, you are more likely to use bullet points (which I deal with on pages 160–3). The semicolon has the drawback of being hard to read on a screen, so it is best avoided on websites.

### Colons

The traditional use of the colon is to tie together two clauses that could stand alone as separate sentences, where the second is an explanation of the first. For example, 'The *Desktop Guide* makes writing easy: it is full of illustrations.' The colon tells the reader that the second clause illustrates the idea expressed in the first.

A much more common use for the colon is to introduce a list, as in 'The *Desktop Guide* helps you with all aspects of writing for the Web: the peculiarities of the Web, the purpose of your website, etc.' So you will often use a colon to introduce bullet points.

## Dashes

The dash is used at the end of a sentence to make an impact. Rather than write 'We know what the result will be. It will be a disaster', you make a more dramatic statement if you write 'We know what the result will be – disaster.' It's a useful device for summing up at the end of a sentence, though if you use it in that way it means you must have written a pretty long sentence. Don't fall into the trap, as some writers do, of using the dash as an all-purpose punctuation mark. It is not a substitute for a full stop, nor usually for a comma or either of the marks in between. Keep it for a specific purpose and it will be effective. Using a lot of dashes on a website makes the pages look messy.

Dashes are also used in abbreviated phrases such as 'Monday–Friday' or figures such as '£10–20 million'. In such phrases the dash stands for the word 'to', so you should write either '£10–20 million' or 'between £10 and £20 million', but not a mixture of the two.

## Hyphens

A hyphen is not the same as a dash. The dash creates a dramatic pause because, except in abbreviated phrases, it has space around it. The hyphen ties words together: it has no space around it. Too many dashes confuse the eye; well placed hyphens help the eye read the text correctly.

There are lots of anecdotes to illustrate the importance of hyphens. There's 'extra-marital sex', which without a hyphen would mean more sex within marriage. There's the story about the company that forgot its hyphens when ordering rods: instead of 'six-foot-long rods', it received 'six foot-long rods'. As you can see from these examples, hyphens are mostly needed when two or more words are turned into an adjective and put before a noun. Those words may have started out as a verb. When you 'set up' a business, you don't need a hyphen, but when you refer to 'set-up costs', you do.

When you talk about private money for projects in the public sector, you may refer to 'projects financed by private money' or 'privately financed projects'. Neither phrase needs punctuation because the structure makes the meaning unambiguous. In the latter, 'privately' is an adverb modifying the verb 'financed', so needs no hyphen. If, however, you refer to 'private-sector finance', you have used the phrase 'private sector' as a single adjective, so you need a hyphen to tie the two words together.

Hyphens are particularly helpful in writing where definitions are of the essence, as in science or medicine. If you describe a mammal as a 'small fish eater', the reader needs to know whether it is small and eats fish or eats only small fish. A non-specialist would find it hard to understand 'high-speed fibre-optic rings' without hyphens. In medical writing it is important to ascribe causes correctly, as in 'cancer-related ailments', and to avoid ambiguity, as in 'patient-friendly contraception'.

## Slashes

With the medium of the computer and the Web came a new punctuation mark known as the slash. There's the back slash, as in 'c:\My Documents\ Desktop Guide' and the forward slash, as in 'www.website.co.uk/services'. In fact it's not a new mark, just a new use of an old mark usually known as the 'oblique' or 'stroke'. The oblique in text is always a forward slash and it's a useful form of shorthand. So we may use it to replace the word 'or' as in 'outer/inner' and, in more technical writing, to replace the Latin word 'per', as in feet/second. The oblique is part of other recognized abbreviations such as '%' for 'per cent', 'c/o' for 'care of', 'i/c' for 'in charge' and '14/5/07' for '14th May 2007'.

The number of different ways you can write dates brings us back to the importance of deciding how you are going to use such abbreviations, and using them consistently.

## Apostrophes

The apostrophe has two functions. It indicates possession, as in 'John's computer' and it indicates where words have been contracted to leave letters out, as in 'don't' for 'do not'. If you are confused by the apostrophe, you are not alone. One reason for confusion is that although the apostrophe indicates possession in nouns, it is not used in possessive pronouns, many of which end in 's'. So it is not used in 'yours', 'his', 'hers', 'its', 'ours' or 'theirs'. One tip for remembering that rule is to think of these pronouns as a group. You wouldn't think of putting an apostrophe in 'mine', or in 'his', so don't put one in 'its'.

The other place you should not put an apostrophe is in a simple plural. Again, confusion arises because we mostly use the letter 's' to make a noun plural. 'Books', 'potatoes' and 'websites' don't need apostrophes. Just occasionally you may need to use them to prevent words being misread. 'Mind your p's and q's' is a rare case where apostrophes in plurals are justified. Another is 'do's and don'ts', and it's a good example of putting the purpose above the rule. Without an apostrophe, the first word might be read as 'doss', but a second apostrophe in 'don'ts' would confuse rather than clarify. There is no consistency here: what matters is that people read the words right first time.

### Quotation marks

The last punctuation marks we deal with are quotation marks or inverted commas. The *Desktop Guide* uses lots of quotation marks, because I have illustrated my advice as much as possible. That raises questions about how to punctuate the examples. Where the quotation is a sentence or more, I have put it into an indented paragraph, but without quotation marks. Short quotations I have kept within a paragraph and put in quotation marks.

I've used single quotation marks rather than double, again to avoid cluttering the text. On a website, however, I recommend double quotation marks because the definition of text on the screen is so much poorer than it is on paper. Whichever style you start with, if you have to quote within a quotation, use the other style within the quotation. It's not a good idea to use inverted commas to indicate sarcasm. Trying to replicate the tone of someone's voice doesn't usually work. If you find yourself waggling your fingers in the air to show that you are quoting, it probably means you are not comfortable with the words you are using and should think again.

## The finishing touch

Punctuation is one of the devices at your disposal to help make up for the deficiencies of writing, as opposed to speaking, as a means of communication. But it should be the finishing touch. Try to make your choice of words and the order you put them in do as much work as possible. Use only those punctuation marks that are necessary to make your meaning clear. On a screen, text is mostly briefer and more broken up than on a printed page and punctuation marks tend to make it look untidy.

## Checklist

- Punctuation marks tend to make a website look messy. Keep them to a minimum.
- Attention-seeking devices such as capitals and bold work only if you use them sparingly.
- Full stops mark the ends of sentences. Dashes or commas won't do.
- Ellipsis (…) means words have been left out. Most other uses are sloppy.
- Commas mark pauses in sentences and separate items in lists.
- Pairs of commas, dashes or brackets (parentheses) mark off inessential material.
- Semicolons mark stronger pauses than commas, but don't show up well on a screen.
- Colons are mostly used to introduce lists.
- A single dash can create a dramatic pause at the end of a sentence.
- Hyphens help the reader by tying the right words together.
- Slashes or obliques are used in certain abbreviations.
- Apostrophes indicate possession or show that letters have been left out.
- Quotation marks are for quoting, and should not be used ironically.

**Part Three
Putting it into
Practice**

# How does it look?

This chapter helps you make the best use of the words on your website. We look at layout in general, and at columns, alignment, fonts, colours, paragraphs, headings and subheadings in particular. We are straying into design, but as a writer you need to know how to present your words and get your message across most effectively.

Research that tracks the eye movements of Web users suggests that they tend to look for words rather than images. Furthermore, users manage to ignore altogether some images that are designed to attract their attention, and even ignore bits of information that look like advertisements, but aren't. Eye-tracking research has also shown where most users look when they scan a page for information. The results remind writers of the importance of presenting their words in the best possible way.

## Where to write

Because our language reads from left to right and top to bottom, we expect text to start somewhere on the left near the top. That is where your most

**Figure 11** This 'heatmap' of a page of search results shows that users concentrate of the top left part of the screen. (Image reproduced courtesy of Eyetools Inc.)

important words should go. It is hardly surprising that eye-tracking research shows that users focus their attention on the left near the top of the screen, but it is worth stating the obvious because so many people ignore it.

Some of your screen will be taken up with navigation. Unlike a book, newspaper or other printed publication, a website has to have navigation on every page to help the user understand the site and the navigation usually goes across the top or down the left side, or both. The right side of the screen may not be visible to the user at first, and you want the user to get your message without having to scroll across or down. That leaves an area of roughly 12×15 centimetres, or 30 square inches, for you to write in.

## How to lay out the words

It is not a good idea to make the text run right across the screen. The longer the line of text, the more the eye has to move. The more the eye has to move, the more difficulty it has finding its way from the end of one line to the beginning of the next. The screen is wider than a page of most books: it is 'landscape' rather than 'portrait'. Some websites, such that in Figure 12, even block out the sides of the screen with a background colour and use only the middle, so that their text looks as if it is on a printed page. In wide books, the text is usually confined to the middle with space on either side or to one side with illustrations on the other. The pages of newspapers and magazines are wider still, but they are divided into columns.

**Figure 12** A website may be easier to read in
'portrait' format than in the usual 'landscape'.

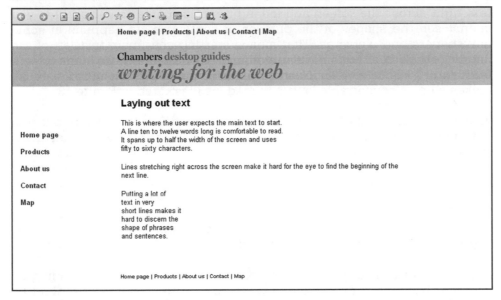

**Figure 13** Text should be laid out in a way that is comfortable to read.

Devices such as columns make it easy for the eye to take in information with as little movement as possible. When you read, you mostly recognize whole words rather than read every letter. If you read fast, you recognize whole phrases or even sentences. There is a happy medium between running the text right across the screen and forcing it into columns so narrow that you cannot see the shapes of the phrases or sentences, as happens in some newspapers and websites. That means starting your main text left of the middle of the screen and making it not more than half the width of the screen. Between 10 and 12 words, or roughly 50 to 60 characters (including spaces), makes a line a comfortable length to read, as illustrated in Figure 13.

Your main text should be somewhere in the middle of the screen, but it is better not centred. Centred text produces messy lists and lines that are hard to read, because each line starts and ends in a different place, as you can see in Figure 14. Research suggests that we read most easily when every line of text starts at the same point on an imaginary line down the left side of the column or page. Text laid out in this way is described as 'left-aligned'. Text can also be 'right-aligned', with every line ending at the same point on an imaginary line down the right side. Lists or lines of text that are right-aligned can be hard to read, because each line starts in a different place.

It is tempting to make the text both left- and right-aligned, as in traditional printing, because it looks tidy. Text laid out in this way is described as 'justified'. But in traditional printing words are carefully hyphenated to fit the width of the column or page, whereas justification in most word processors varies the spaces between letters and words to fit the width. This stretching and compressing of words confuses the eye. My advice is to align your text on the left and leave it ragged on the right, as in Figure 15.

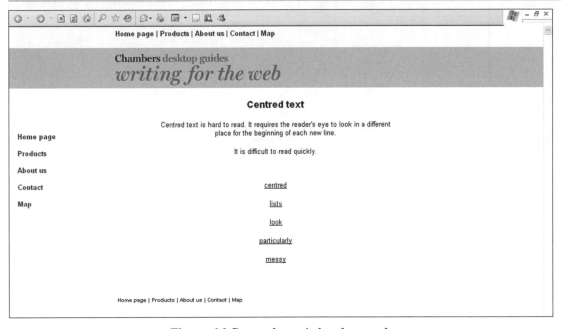

**Figure 14** Centred text is hard to read.

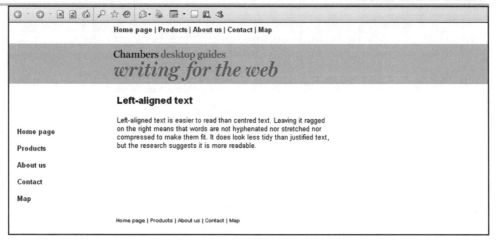

**Figure 15** Left-aligned text is the easiest to read.

## Fonts

My advice about fonts is also based on research into how people read most easily. In general, the eye finds it easier to read fonts with serifs, like Times, the serif being the little bit added to the top left and bottom right of most letters. The serifs have the effect of leading the eye from the end of one letter to the beginning of the next. In print, serif fonts are used for the majority of text. On a screen, other considerations come into play. The screen uses fewer dots per inch than print. Letters are much less clearly defined. So the serif fonts, rather than helping the eye, may burden it by looking fuzzy.

Most professionally designed websites use fonts without serifs, sans-serif fonts, such as Arial. The general rule has come to be: serif for print, sans-serif for screen. But it is not as simple as that. Many sans-serif fonts were developed for headlines or posters and were not intended for text. If your site has relatively little text and that text is in small chunks, sans-serif will work well. But if you have a lot of text and especially if you expect the user to print what you have written rather than read it on screen, your text will be easier to read in a serif font.

Sites with a lot of text often compromise, as do many printed texts. They use a sans-serif font for the headings, subheadings and navigation where the user is scanning the page for the key information, and a serif font for the body of the text where the user has focused his or her attention and wants to read. Many websites get round the problem by making separate versions of pages that users are likely to want to print and read on paper. The printer-friendly version can be in a serif font. If you make a printer-friendly version, you can go further and strip out all but the minimum information needed to identify the site as the source of the text, leaving maximum space for the text the user is interested in. Making printer-friendly pages on your website shows that you are thinking of what the user wants.

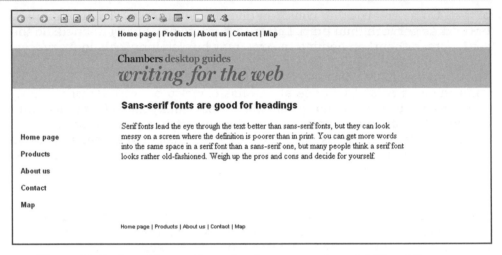

**Figure 16** Choice of fonts affects the character and readability of the page.

Apart from functional considerations, there's the character of a font. Your choice of font says something about you and what you are offering on your website. Successful sites tend to be those with a distinct personality. You might not use the same font to sell computer accessories as you would to discuss antiques or compare different ways of planting a vegetable garden. In the end you will weigh up all these considerations, try different fonts on screen and make a judgment for yourself. Once you've decided, stick to your decision. A site that uses several different fonts looks messy and unprofessional.

## Colour

Your choice of colours is for the most part beyond the scope of this book, but as a writer you have an interest in your words being as clear as possible on the screen. You need to have your own ideas as to what works and what doesn't, and there are some aspects that are relevant when deciding how to present what you write.

The clearest text to read is in black letters on a white background. That is too dull for many people, but the rule must be to make your font and background colours as distinct from one another as you can. Quite a few sites use white text on a black background. Some use white on a strong colour. It depends what counts as strong. White on green is reckoned all right; white on red is not. Unfortunately I can't show you here, but look at some sites yourself to see what works.

Just as you need to be consistent in your use of words and fonts, so you should ensure that your site uses colours consistently. Nearly every site uses a colour for its links and if no colour is specified, they will come out blue. It helps the user if the same colour is used for links throughout the site, so that every text link looks the same and behaves the same. Links should change colour once they have been used, so that users, especially first-time visitors to your site, know which links they have already tried.

Some sites use colour-coding to distinguish different areas of a page or whole sections of the site. This can work, provided there is some logic behind it. Alternating background colours on alternating items, just for the sake of it, may confuse the user; whereas having a different background colour or a different coloured heading for each category of information can be helpful.

### Combining text and images

As human beings we react to pictures of other human beings, especially faces. But pictures of no-one in particular, put on a website to make it look more interesting, use up precious space and may even put users off because they suggest the site is more of a glossy brochure than a source of useful information. On most sites, you should use pictures (images) to convey information rather than merely a mood. To make your site accessible to as many users as possible, you should always write alternative ('alt') text to go with the images so that users waiting for them to load, or users who can't see them, know what is in them. If you also write captions that appear beside or below the images on the page, as in Figure 17, your pictures will be all the more informative.

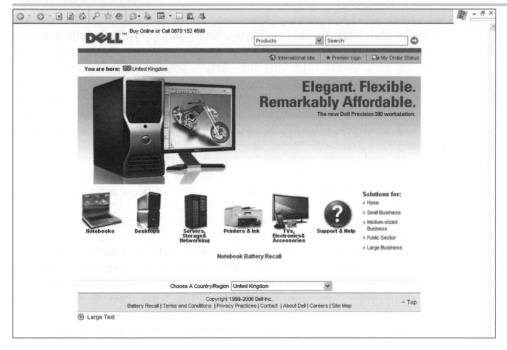

**Figure 17** Images and text working together to provide useful information.

Having to write captions makes you think about why you are using this particular image and whether it conveys the message you intended. If you find yourself having to put a lot of information into a caption, the image is probably not conveying enough. Similarly if you find yourself writing a caption that has little to do with the picture or even contradicts what's in it, then you've got the wrong image. Make the caption complement the image. Don't tell sighted users what they can see for themselves, but rather supply additional information such as names of people and places, or some background detail.

When it comes to using other images, especially charts and graphs, text is vital. A chart or graph without explanatory text is uninformative, and in some cases dishonest.

### Making the text easy to scan

Since the early days of the Web, it has been clear that users scan pages on a website rather than reading every word. Eye-tracking research suggests they scan a page in an F pattern: they read from the left across some of the text near the top, then down the left, reading across perhaps one more line, and then scanning down the left hand side. Again, it may be stating the obvious to say that people scan mainly down the left of a page to decide whether the text is what they are looking for, but we need constantly to remind ourselves of the value of signposts such as headings and subheadings, and of the need to put the important words at the start of every paragraph, heading and subheading.

## i. Paragraphs

We break up text to make it easier to take in. The way we break it up reflects the way we have organized the information we are offering. Many Victorian novels were divided into chapters equivalent to the amount of text that a man might read to his family in an evening or the amount that made a coherent chunk of narrative when the novel appeared in instalments in a magazine. That meant chapters of similar length consisting of dense text usually appearing under a single heading.

There is no standard unit for dividing text on a website. The information is broken up into many pieces of many different lengths, from three-word headings to many-thousand-word articles, depending on where you are in the hierarchy of the site. Though there are different considerations on different pages, on most pages the rule of thumb might be to write paragraphs of 25-35 words, or roughly 140-220 characters.

What makes a paragraph easy to identify is not the words in it but the space around it. In print that is called white space and for some this term has carried over into websites, even though the space may be yellow or black. The amount of white space will depend on where you are in the hierarchy of the site: there will usually be more on the home page and the pages immediately below it, and less in the lower, more detailed pages.

You need space on either side of text, in the form of margins, and you will usually put space between paragraphs. For years, the convention in printing was to indent paragraphs, to start each new paragraph several spaces in from the left. That works well in dense continuous text: you look for the space at the start of the indented line to see where a new paragraph starts. The introduction of word processing, however, allowed almost anyone, not just professional printers, to publish documents. We all began to play around with layout and to use paper quite profligately. With more white space on the page, indenting paragraphs does not work so well. It is now usual instead to put a line space between paragraphs and to align the first word of each paragraph to the left, as in this book.

On a website, it is vital for the eye to be able to identify the main elements of the information quickly. Finding the start of paragraphs is one of the key ways of doing this. Putting margins on either side of your paragraphs and a line space between them makes each paragraph stand out as a block. Rather than having to look along the first line for the indentation, it is easier for the eye to find the start of the paragraph at the top left corner of each block.

Blocks of text look easier to read than continuous prose. By taking the trouble to divide your text up, you show that you are trying to help the reader. But it's not an arbitrary division. There is an interplay between the visual requirements and the organization of your thoughts. Having to divide your text into paragraphs makes you think about the way your information is structured. Each paragraph should have a single topic. A paragraph may consist of a single sentence or many, but in a website they will usually be two or three sentences long.

## ii. Headings

When text is dense and justified, as it is in many books and magazines, it makes sense to centre the title or page heading to make it stand out above the text. Where text is broken up by a lot of white space, however, a centred heading can look lost. I have recommended that you align your text on the left and leave it ragged on the right. The same applies with the heading. If you align your heading with the text, you are creating a vertical line on which each new bit of information starts, so making it easier for the user to read what you write. A heading may be a single word or as much as seven words long. What matters is how it looks in relation to the text below it. Whatever the width of your text, the heading should not take up more than one line, otherwise it loses impact.

## iii. Subheadings

Not all websites use subheadings, and in this book not every paragraph has a subheading above it, but subheadings help users as they scan the page for information. Subheadings should be written so as to provide a list of contents. They may consist of a single word or two or three. For visual impact they should be less than half the width of the text they sit above. As well as helping the user scan the page, they help you, the writer, clarify your thoughts. Having to use subheadings makes you think, 'What is this particular paragraph about?'

**Checklist**

- You have an area less than half the size of the screen to write in.
- The prime position is left of centre near the top.
- Your text should be no more than half the width of the screen.
- Centred text is hard to read, as is right-aligned and justified text.
- Text that is left-aligned and ragged on the right is easiest to read.
- Serif fonts are easier to read on paper, but sans-serif fonts look better on a screen.
- Text and background colours should be as distinct from one another as possible.
- Writing 'alt' text and captions helps users and makes your images more informative.
- Paragraphs, headings and subheadings should be left-aligned.
- Dividing your text into paragraphs forces you to structure your information.
- Writing subheadings above paragraphs makes your text easy to scan.

# Stories, summaries, headlines and lists

This chapter deals with four of the key skills in Web writing: writing stories, summaries, headlines and lists. It develops the idea that Web writing has a lot in common with news writing and suggests ways of practising the skills described.

## What kind of stories?

I said on page 79 that good writing was like telling stories. On the Web, that is only partly true. You should try to write about real people doing things, about events that your reader can visualize. But you are not writing traditional stories like the epic poems of Homer or the novels of Jane Austen. You cannot afford to write an intriguing introduction, keep your readers waiting a couple of chapters before introducing the hero and expect people to read three hundred pages to the end of the story to find out what happens to him. Web writing does not necessarily have a beginning, a middle and an end.

The writer of a scientific paper usually starts by explaining how the research came to be done and the methods and terms used, and goes on to describe the process of discovery chronologically. To other scientists, the methods used are often the most important part of the paper because unless the methods stand up to scrutiny the conclusions of an experiment will not be valid. As in a novel, the conclusion comes at the end.

In news writing, this order is reversed: the conclusion or climax comes first. The journalist puts the most important information at the top of the story, followed by the other facts or explanations in decreasing order of importance. Because the structure of scientific writing is said to be like a pyramid, news writing is often described as an inverted pyramid.

Newspaper articles are written in this way so that an editor can cut the story from the bottom to fit the available space, confident that the most important part will still be published. Writing for the Web is like writing news in that the important information must come first. Many users won't scroll down. They will look at the first paragraph, perhaps read the first few words and decide quickly whether to bother with the rest.

As a Web writer, you need to go one stage further than the writer of a news story. Not only should you put the important information at the top of anything you write, you should always try to give users only as much information as they want at any particular point. If they are interested in what you say in the first paragraph, they can read more detail in the next few paragraphs or via links. They should not have to waste time reading what doesn't interest them to find what they want. That is why summaries, headlines and lists are so important on a website. They are the means of leading users in easy stages to what they want.

### The process of writing

Whatever you have to write, you need a method. It can be quite daunting to be faced with a big writing job. One way of making it easier is to divide the process into stages. The first is to gather your source material. This may be all in one form, such as a written report or article. It may be your memory of a conversation with one or more people, or notes from such a conversation or meeting. It may be a recording of an interview or something you are going to review. It may be a mixture of any of these. If you are going to tell someone else about it, you need to understand it yourself.

Ideally, when you write, you should use the raw material rather than a version that has already been digested by someone else – a PR person, for example, or a news agency journalist – who may have reasons for interpreting it in a certain way. Such versions are intended to sell the material to a customer and often include persuasive introductions that are not borne out by the body of the report. In real life, it is often impossible to go back to original sources. We simply don't have time, but it is worth bearing in mind what these versions are – someone else's version.

When you have gathered your material, go through it for a general idea of what it is about. It is probably better not to take notes at this stage as you want to get a sense of it as a whole. When you have got the gist, make a few notes from memory. Then go through it again carefully, making notes, underlining or using a highlighter pen. Think what points you want to include and in what order. Plan what you are going to say.

Make sure your plan is complete. It is often easy to think of a good way to start and then what comes next, without thinking where it is all going. You need to know how you are going to end before you start writing, because you need a sense of direction through the whole piece. To take a simple example, you would not start writing an email in reply to an invitation before you had decided whether to accept or not. If you did, your email would probably ramble as you rehearsed the pros and cons. Once you had decided, your email would come out differently according to whether the answer was Yes or No.

The better you plan your writing, the better the result is likely to be. It is hard to resist the desire to get on with it, but it is worth putting off writing until you are ready; then the writing itself will go more quickly and smoothly.

When I was learning to write news, I was encouraged to put the source material away and write from memory. I still find it the best method. Writing from memory makes you assess and digest the information before you write. You then write confidently and produce a more natural, flowing piece because you are using your own words and keeping the shape of the whole piece in your head. Writing with your source material around you can produce a cut-and-paste job that is stilted and unsatisfactory, because you tend to use other people's words, and your attention is on details so you can easily lose the thread of the piece. If you need to consult the source material to quote something accurately, you can always mark your draft and carry on writing. When you have finished, you can go back to check that quotation or fact.

The last stage is revising and editing. Whatever you write, don't be satisfied with the first draft. Allow time for editing. There's a lot you can do to improve your draft by going through it carefully, clarifying any ambiguities, removing unnecessary words and phrases and rewriting whole sentences if necessary.

## Structuring stories

Start with a strong first sentence. That's easy to say, but how do you decide what the most important information is? Another journalist's device that you can use is a list of simple questions to answer: What?, Where?, When?, Who?, Why? and How? When you have gathered your information, jot down the bare bones as answers to each of those questions. If, for example, you are promoting a conference, jot down what it is, where and when it will happen, who it's for and who will be speaking, why it has been organized and how people can take part. Then you can decide the order of importance of the various bits of information with your target users in mind.

Breaking up the information into its basic elements will help you structure your story. In some stories, the person or people involved are the most important element and you will put them first. In others, the most important element may be what happened, and in others it may be the place or the time. It is hard to rearrange information once you have written whole sentences and paragraphs. Seeing your story as made up of separate elements makes it easier to get the information into the right order for your purpose and your audience, before you start writing.

### Summaries

If you have articles, documents or large bodies of information on your website, you need to be able to provide users with a summary of what is in them, so that they don't waste time reading a lot of irrelevant material. One writer giving advice on writing summaries used the provocative title Make Sure Nobody Reads Your News. He meant that if your summaries are good, users won't need to read the full stories to know what is going on.

Summing up an article or document in a few words is another daunting task. You will do it best if you thoroughly understand the material you are summarizing and if you write from memory. Imagine someone asking you what it's about and make yourself tell them in two or three sentences.

There's a danger that in summarizing you lose the elegance of the original, the detail and the colour. A summary that consists of generalizations is boring and uninformative. Lists of specifics can also be boring and hard to take in. Try to use an element of both – a general point with something specific that illustrates it. The general point tells readers what you are talking about and the specific gives them something they can visualize or identify with.

Practise summing up information in two sentences, say 30 words. That makes a nice short paragraph on a Web page.

Writing summaries is something journalists do all the time. The advantage journalists have is less their talent or their training – important though these are – and more their daily practice and the criticism they get from editors and colleagues. The more you write and the more feedback you get on what you write, the better your writing is likely to be. Writing headlines is another journalistic skill that is essential for good Web writing. It, too, needs practice.

## Headlines

Whereas a summary tells you what the story is, a headline tells you what is interesting about it. Headlines are sometimes described as enticing a reader into a story. There is a difference between enticing and teasing. A teaser does not tell you much and often does not deliver what it promises. This is annoying in any circumstances. On a website it can be disastrous, as users lose patience very quickly. Put yourself in their position. If you buy a newspaper or magazine, you are prepared to make some effort to read it. After all, you chose it and paid for it. Users have made no such decision about your site. They are investing their time, and it takes far more time and effort to look around a site than it does to find what you want in a magazine.

A headline encourages the user to read a story. Headlines on websites have to work harder than they do in print. In newspapers and magazines, headlines often appear above the stories they refer to. On a website they are usually on a separate page acting as links to the stories or to summaries. Your headlines have to be interesting enough to persuade the user to follow a link to another page and risk getting lost in your site.

To write an interesting headline, first think of a person you want to interest. Imagine yourself ringing someone up to give them some useful information or going home to someone quite unconnected with your work and being asked about it, or talking to a stranger. Imagine yourself in a group where you have to take your turn in the conversation and you have a very short time to capture the interest of the most important person there. Whichever way is most helpful, try always to visualize an individual and think what would be interesting, new and relevant to him or her.

There are several devices you can use. You can offer practical help as in 'How to get the best service from us'. Headlines that start with 'How to ...' work because as readers we like to feel we are getting something useful. You can use a figure or a statistic, as in '40% of the food we eat is worthless'.

Figures attract our interest perhaps because they are easy to take in and they sound so definite. You can combine two devices in one headline, as in 'Three reasons for having your widgets cleaned regularly', offering useful advice in a form that sounds easy to take in. You can ask a question: that gets the reader's attention, but it becomes tiresome if you do it too much. You can see some examples in Figure 18.

You can adapt familiar phrases to make a joke or a pun. Puns are a favourite device of headline-writers, but at the risk of sounding stuffy, my advice is to avoid jokes and puns. That doesn't mean never use them; just don't try too hard. Jokes and puns make a lot of assumptions about the people you are writing for: that they have similar experiences, knowledge and sense of humour – in other words a similar culture. Such headlines are often appreciated by people who don't get the allusion, but that's because they sound good anyway. Your effort should go into writing something that sounds interesting. If you manage a joke or pun, it's a bonus.

It is usually better to write the headline after you have written the story. We may think of a clever headline and then find that the story we have written doesn't match the headline. In practice it doesn't much matter which order you write them in, provided you remember to read the headline again afterwards to check that it fits the story. Starting with a headline, at least in mind, is often a way of launching ourselves into a story because it provides an angle. It gets us going.

**Figure 18** Examples of enticing headlines.

Is the headline the same as the first sentence of the story? No. The first sentence is part of the story and will be written accordingly. It is rather boring to read a headline and then find that the first sentence of the story is exactly the same. The headline, ideally written afterwards, stands alone and should give the flavour of the story, the reason for reading it. The headline does not itself have to be a sentence, but it will be more informative if it is. It does have to be short; otherwise it loses impact.

Headlines on one page should make sense as a group. In that, they are rather like the table of contents in this book. Having written the chapters, I went back to the Contents to see if the chapter headings made sense as a list. They had to be roughly the same length, and short but informative. They had to convey a sense of progress from the introduction to the conclusion. They had to form a balanced whole, being neither repetitive nor mismatched, not sounding as though they were put together in bits at different stages, but written as a set.

On a website your set of headlines will tend to be much shorter than the table of contents of a book, but they must make sense as a set, as well as represent the information to which they refer. This applies to subheadings too. If you put subheadings above your paragraphs, the subheadings should not only give the flavour of each paragraph, but also make a coherent list, in effect a list of the contents of the page.

## Lists

In our search for ways of writing pages that the user can easily scan for information, we have discussed how to break up text into paragraphs, how to write summaries, headlines and subheadings, and how to make lists of headlines and subheadings. Now we'll look at two of the most useful devices on a website: lists of links and bullet points.

It's worth spending a little time thinking about how lists work. Putting information in a list is a way of making a lot of information accessible in a short time. A list can consist of almost anything: departments of an organization, people in those departments, hobbies, actions required, qualities in a person, types of products, and so on. The important characteristic of a list is that the items in it should all be of the same type.

A shopping list consists of objects that you need to buy. If you put down apples, oranges and potatoes, you have a coherent list of things you will probably buy in one place. If you add a newspaper and some light bulbs, you may have to go to different places to buy them, but you are still dealing with things to buy. If you add new wallpaper for the bedroom, you are still dealing with something to buy, but it will presumably need more time and thought than buying potatoes. If you then add 'Book dental appointment' and 'Must remember to ask Jo about the sunflowers', you are liable to get confused. Putting all these things in the same list makes it hard to use. You may well sort the items into separate lists. Alternatively, you may say, 'It's my list, I know what it means.'

If you were to ask someone else to do your shopping, however, you would think far more carefully about what to put on the list and how you described those things. You know which newspaper you usually buy; someone else may not. You know when an appointment would suit you; someone else would not. On a website, your lists are all drawn up for someone else – the user. Lists of links are like shopping lists in that they are there for the user to act on. What is more, the user does not necessarily understand at first glance what a list is for, unless you make this clear. This is hard when your lists are made up of single words, as are many lists of links.

I mentioned lists in the chapter about organizing your site. I said on page 37 that three items were the minimum needed to make a list. If you write down two things, another person may see a connection between them, but it takes a third item to confirm that they have made the right connection. Most people can keep about seven items in their head at once. If your list goes up to nine or ten, you are making it hard for the user to understand what you are offering. Once you have more than seven items, you should think about putting them into separate categories.

Many lists you see on websites make no sense to the user. The items are in the order of their importance to the owner of the site rather than the user.

Even when sites put items in the order they think they are most likely to be used, the logic is not necessarily obvious, certainly not to the first-time user. Besides, individual users may have different reasons for coming to your site and may be looking for different things. There is a lot to be said for making lists alphabetical, especially when you have a lot of categories and a lot of items in each category. At least the user can understand at a glance how they work and may then feel more comfortable looking to see what they contain.

### Bullet points

Breaking up text into bulleted lists is only a little easier than writing lists of links. Putting a mark in front of short bits of text and putting the bits on separate lines may make the page look orderly, but the bullet points won't work unless the contents have been carefully thought out. Keep in mind the idea of a shopping list. That will focus your attention on the things to be listed rather than the appearance of a list.

Badly written bullet points are those that are not real lists, because they consist of things that are not the same and so cannot be understood at a glance. You can see an example in Figure 19. They will be more difficult to read than a well written paragraph. Real lists consist of ideas expressed in the same way. That means using the same part of speech – five nouns or noun phrases, for example, or five adjectives. A list of things to do would consist of verbs, 'fetch dry cleaning, book appointment with dentist, check

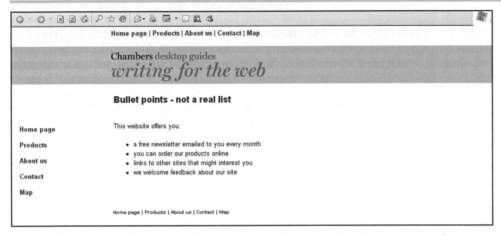

**Figure 19** Bullet points that are not real lists are hard to understand.

diaries with Sarah, order paper for printer', all expressed as commands. If you were to add a fifth item, 'I must remember to ring Mum', it would no longer be a real list, but if you changed that item to 'ring Mum' it would.

Items in a bulleted list may be short sentences, but they usually work best if they are single words or phrases, with an introduction. Try to start each item in the list – and this applies to links as well – with a strong word and one which is different from the others. Take some time to practise converting text into bullet points. You will often find that one item doesn't fit with the others and you will need to rewrite that item or some or all of the others. Make sure that every item fits your introduction, as in Figure 20. It is easy to start a list well and, by the time you get to the fourth item, to forget what you said in your introduction.

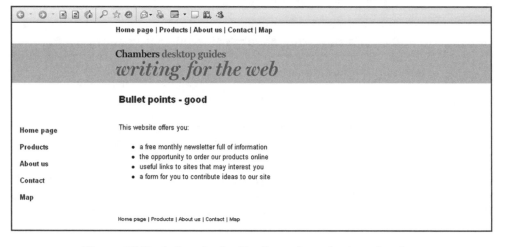

**Figure 20** Each item in the list flows from the introduction.

As the purpose of a bulleted list is to enable the user to scan a lot of information in a small space, your items should not go over one line. Bullet points should be of similar length and unpunctuated to look tidy and be easy to scan. I suggest that they should start in lower case, unless of course they are proper names. The reason is that the bullet, like the capital letter, is a device for drawing attention. If you use two such devices at once, you tend to confuse the reader.

Finally, the bullet is a powerful visual device but not necessarily the right choice for every kind of information. Make sure that the information you put in a bulleted list is really important and not just the bits that are easy to put into a list; otherwise you will distort your message. Don't try to use bullets when you are weighing up advantages and disadvantages: bullets are no good for presenting arguments. And don't use bullets when you should be using numbers. If your items are in order, as in the case of instructions, use numbers: they won't look as pretty as bullets but they will be more helpful to the user.

## Checklist

- Web writing has more in common with news writing than with traditional story-telling.
- Always put the important information first.
- Read through your source material, make notes and plan what you are going to say.
- Write from memory to ensure that your writing flows.
- A mixture of general points and specific examples makes a good summary.
- Headlines should arouse the user's interest in a story, without misleading.
- On websites, headlines have to work harder than they do in print: they often stand alone.
- Visualize the person you are trying to interest; write something relevant to them.
- Avoid jokes and puns.
- Headlines on one page should make sense as a set.
- Any list should consist of items of the same type and be easy to scan.
- Lists of links must make sense to the user.
- Bullet points should be real lists and lists of important things.

# Writing pages with a purpose

You can't be sure where a user will land in your site, so you need to write every page as well as you can, and that means keeping in mind its particular purpose. I start with what is good practice for all pages and then give you some thoughts about particular types of page.

## Engage the user

Test some sites at random. Which did you find you really wanted to use? The answer is often the ones with a clear identity; you might say with 'personality'. They make you feel there are real people in there somewhere, and that the site is meant for you or someone like you. As a writer, you need to engage the other person in the dialogue – the user. The more clearly you can visualize your typical user, the better the conversation you will be able to construct. You will choose the right words to communicate with that person.

## Put your best bits first

You have so little space to work with on a Web page. You may find that the space you are working with is even smaller than you first thought. The top of

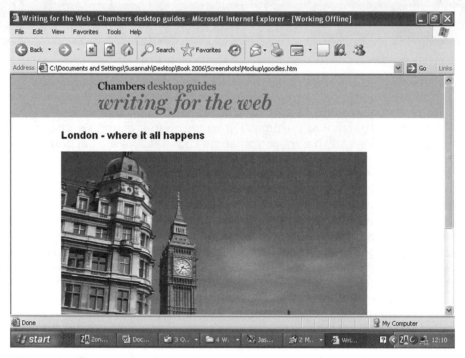

**Figure 21** The appearance of a page will vary according to the screen set-up. What do you think this website is about? (Image: freeimages.co.uk)

**Figure 22** Is this what you were expecting the website to be about from Figure 21?
(Image: freeimages.co.uk)

the screen will be filled by the browser's menu bar and some of the top, or one side – or both – will be taken up with navigation. It's worth remembering that people use different-sized screens, some users will not have the screen maximized and many will not bother to scroll. Other users may be looking at mobile devices with a limited screen size. All your important words must appear near the top of the page. The prime space on a newspaper page is 'above the fold'. On a Web page, it is vital that your key messages are 'above the line'. Figures 21 and 22 show how different a website can look when viewed on different screens.

## Write good links

Writing 'Click here' is frowned on by many Web experts. You want to be helpful to inexperienced users, but you should consider several objections to this device. Some users don't use a mouse and therefore don't click at all. Another objection is that it wastes words: even if users don't want to follow that link, they can still gain information from it. A third objection is on visual grounds. Links that say 'Click here' draw attention to the wrong words. If you have several of them on a page, as in Figure 23, the user scanning for information sees repeated instances of 'here' or 'click', instead of the categories of information you are offering.

The better you have planned your site to anticipate what the user wants, the more easily the links will integrate with the text, and the less conscious the user will be of the mechanics of the site. Make your links as specific as

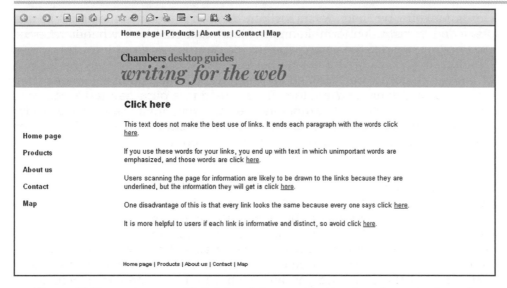

**Figure 23** Excessive use of 'click here' draws attention to unimportant words.

possible: words like 'solutions' and 'services' are not very informative and are capable of several different interpretations. When users see a link they should have a clear idea what it leads to. Try to make each link unique, so don't use different words in different places for the same link, and don't use the same words for different links. Even a slight difference, such as 'register' in one place and 'registration form' in another, can make the user wonder whether the two links lead to the same page.

Wherever possible your links should match the headings of the pages they lead to. So a link called 'About us' should lead to a page headed 'About us', not 'Who we are'. Again, the difference is not great, but it is enough to briefly disrupt the smooth flow of information from the site to the user. Remember how easily users are confused and disorientated: if they lose confidence in their ability to navigate your site they may give up.

### Place your links

Some Web writers refuse to put links in the text in case the user goes straight to another page and misses the rest of the information in that sentence, paragraph or page. This is less likely if you place your links at the end of sentences and paragraphs, but you have to accept that you cannot dictate to the user. You cannot even guide. You can only offer. Probably the sooner you abandon the idea that you are in charge, the better. Your website is there for the benefit of the user and contextual links answer users' questions as they arise. You should be confident that if you are giving users a good experience, they will come back.

Having links in the text as well as in a list helps to reinforce your navigation. It is a good idea to give the user more than one way of reaching other pages, and putting links in the text gives you an opportunity to explain them. But place them carefully and avoid cluttering the text with too many. The pages of some very successful sites, such as news sites, seem to ignore this advice and consist almost entirely of links in fairly dense text. I think they get away with it because they tend to come from known organizations and use familiar categories of information, and so have less need to explain themselves.

## Always explain

There should be no surprises in a website, except perhaps a few pleasant ones. You need constantly to anticipate users' anxieties by explaining what you are offering and telling them what to expect. So, if you are offering a link to another website, it's a good idea to make that clear; some sites even write out the URL (the full Web address), so that there can be no doubt. If you are offering a download in a format other than a Web page, such as Word®, PowerPoint® or PDF, say so and say how big the file is. Many users will not understand a file size expressed in kilobytes, such as 243K, but if you also tell them it is 45 pages long, they will fairly quickly decide whether they really want it or not. There's an example of a helpful page in Figure 24.

Whenever you suggest that users do something, give them a reason first. This is especially important when you are asking them for information or leading them through a process that requires them to do things right at each stage. If you tell the user why you need a postcode, for example, and what you will do with it, you are much more likely to get it. Most of us are

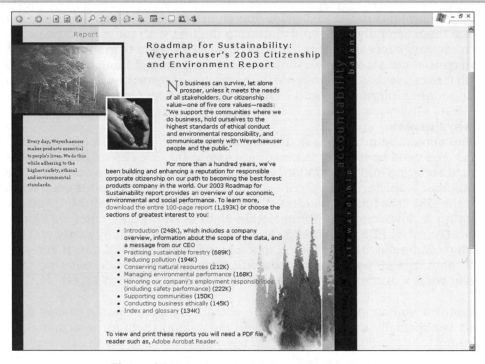

**Figure 24** Help the user by describing content,
format and size of downloads.

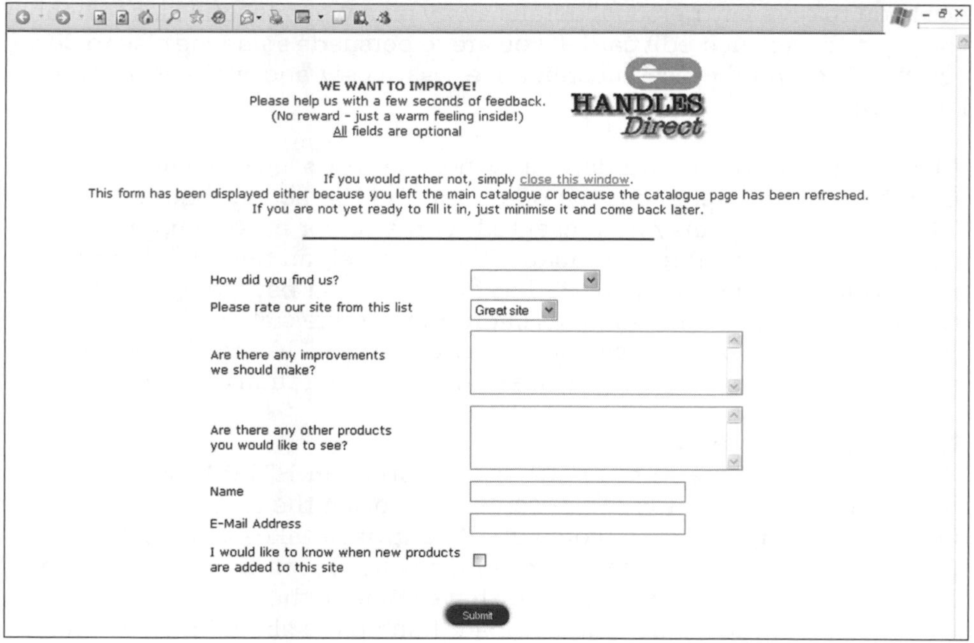

**WE WANT TO IMPROVE!**
Please help us with a few seconds of feedback.
(No reward - just a warm feeling inside!)
<u>All</u> fields are optional

If you would rather not, simply <u>close this window</u>.
This form has been displayed either because you left the main catalogue or because the catalogue page has been refreshed.
If you are not yet ready to fill it in, just minimise it and come back later.

HANDLES Direct

How did you find us?

Please rate our site from this list    Great site

Are there any improvements
we should make?

Are there any other products
you would like to see?

Name

E-Mail Address

I would like to know when new products
are added to this site

Submit

**Figure 25** When you ask users for information,
tell them why and make it easy.

not keen to give any personal details away on a website, still less to enable someone to use our credit card. If you are to persuade someone else to do so, you need to win the user's confidence, ask nicely and make it easy, as in Figure 25.

When you are writing words that either lead to a link or support a link elsewhere on the page, put the offer first and the action required second. Otherwise the user may be presented with a rather mystifying instruction such as 'Press Ctrl+P to print map'. It is more helpful the other way round, as 'To print map press Ctrl + P'. Besides it is good psychology. If the user sees 'Scroll down to see examples of my work', there's always a danger that the response will be 'Why should I?' Saying 'If you'd like to see examples of my work, scroll down' gives the user a choice rather than an order.

### Remember the <title>
The words you write in the page title (<title> in HTML), which appear in the bar at the very top of the screen, are often the first words the user sees when a page starts to come up. If your page takes time to load, they may be the only words the user sees for several seconds, so it's important that they reassure the user that they have come to the right place and that it is worth waiting for the page to load. Each page should have a specific title – not just the name of your organization, but also what that particular page is about.

## The home page

The home page should answer the question 'What will this site do for me?'. A user will probably decide in a couple of seconds whether the site is interesting or not. That decision will be influenced by the look of the page and the speed at which it loads, but research suggests that what the user really looks for is words. Remember that the user cannot see your site in the way that a reader can see and hold and thumb through an entire book or magazine in a few seconds. In the few seconds you have before the user becomes impatient or confused or bored, the words on your home page must do three things: they must identify you and your site; they must make clear what you are offering; and they must help the user find it.

The words you come up with to describe yourself and what you offer will become the key words at the top of your home page and other pages too. The task is to think hard about what makes your site special and to describe it accurately in as few words as possible. It's tempting to put as much on the home page as you can, to show off everything you've got, but that is usually a mistake. Users can't take it all in, and you can't afford to confuse or mislead, or they'll go elsewhere. Figure 26 shows a good example of a clear home page.

Asking people to register on the home page is not the best way to start a conversation. It suggests that you are more interested in getting their details than providing them with something useful or enjoyable. Many organizations,

**Figure 26** A site with clear aims. (© Cancer Research UK. Reproduced with the kind permission of Cancer Research UK.)

such as newspapers, made this mistake when they first went online. They were afraid of losing their existing business and required users to subscribe or at least register before they gave them access to information. They soon realized that, far from losing them business, giving away information online gained them new customers and enhanced their reputation with existing ones.

Successful websites are often those that offer the user the possibility of receiving newsletters, emails or RSS feeds. (RSS feeds are bits of information automatically sent from a site to users who have chosen to receive them.) These may be tailored to individual users' interests, such as stories about particular industries or notice of certain events. This kind of communication creates a relationship between the user and the site.

It is not enough for a home page to impress users the first time they visit. If you want people to visit your site again, you must make it worth their while and give them something new as often as you can. Having some kind of 'news' section on your home page ensures that you cater for repeat visitors as well as first-timers, provided that you are able to update your site fairly often.

In describing what you are offering, you have a few lines in which to persuade the user that you have something he or she wants. Your best chance lies in vivid but factual description, and in writing about your service from the perspective of the user rather than your own. You need also to make clear the limits of what you are offering. If you tell people about the products you make, users may assume they can order them online. If they can't, you need to put in an address or telephone number high up the page, or mention writing or telephoning pretty quickly.

Having told users what they can expect from your site, you need to tell them how to get it. It helps to have a familiar navigation system used by other sites similar to your own. Research suggests that the value of familiarity outweighs the weakness of any particular system of navigation. Refer to the navigation in the text. You can't explain it in detail, but it is important that the home page should be an introduction to both the content and the workings of your site. The text should support the navigation by using the same words as the links, in the same order, and reinforce the ideas represented by them, as in Figure 27.

More and more people use search engines rather than enter a Web address (URL) in their browsers. This means that many users will never see your home page and won't need to because they will have come via a search engine to a page in your website that provides the information they want. So it is important to think carefully about all the other pages. Users may be just as put off by a badly written registration page as a badly written home page.

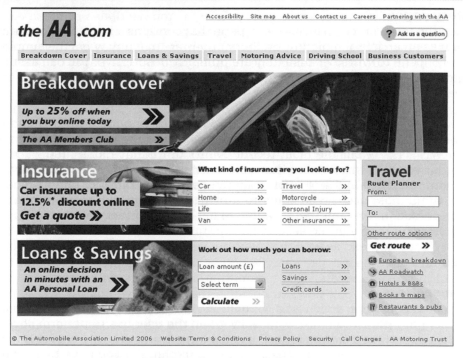

**Figure 27** Use the same words in the same
order in the navigation and the text.

## Story pages

I use the term 'story' to include any page that contains a body of information such as an article or a biography. Story pages are in many ways the simplest kind of page to write because they are primarily descriptive. You can assume that users have chosen to come to this page to find out about a topic or a person and you can just give them the information.

It will not be in traditional story form – with a beginning, a middle and an end. For example, when you are putting a biography onto a single page, you will usually put the most recent events or qualifications first. In other words, you will start with what you think is most interesting or relevant to your audience and add information in decreasing order of importance. If you think most users who come to a biography page will want to contact that person, make sure there's a link to his or her contact details high up in the story, probably in the second paragraph, rather than at the bottom. The 'story' may not read as well that way, but it will be more useful to the people reading it.

## Transactions

Pages that require action and input from the user are probably the most challenging pages to write, especially when the user has to perform several tasks correctly in a certain order. I use the term 'transactions' to cover buying goods, donating money or subscribing to something. If you have been using websites involving transactions for some time, you may have noticed how much some of them have improved. Since it is possible to track users' movements and see exactly where they abandon a transaction, website owners can see where they are losing money and try to do something about it.

An airline, for example, has put the total cost of a flight at the start of the transaction, presumably because users felt deceived at being offered a cheap flight that turned out not to be so cheap once taxes, surcharges and so on had been added. Another website has inserted assurances into the early stages of the transaction to make it clear that no money has yet been paid. Many websites have improved themselves by labelling the stages in the transaction, telling users what each stage involves and letting users know where they are at any time.

If you want users to complete a task, let them focus on that task. Remove all information – navigation, slogans, descriptive material – not directly relevant to the task (see Figure 28). Don't, for example, carry on telling them why they might like to join when they have already decided to. Place instructions as near as possible to the part of the transaction they relate to. It is not very helpful to put a list of instructions down the left-hand side of the page when the actions they refer to are in various places in the middle of the screen. Use terms consistently and make sure that the user will understand what you mean. Even a simple option like 'Continue shopping' is ambiguous: some people use 'shopping' to mean buying things; others to mean looking for things they may or may not buy.

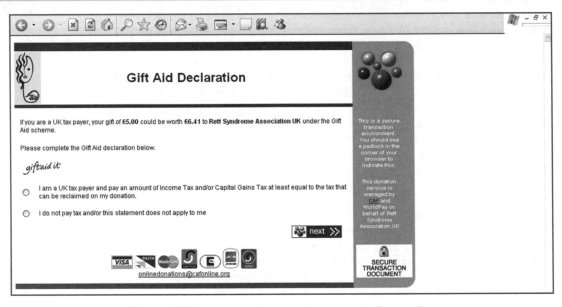

**Figure 28** Let users concentrate on one task at a time.

## Forms

You can find whole websites devoted to the art of designing forms. Forms are vitally important for businesses and organizations, but filling them in is a chore for website users, so try to make it as easy as possible. Think first what you are going to do with the information provided. Your purpose should be something specific, such as to enable a user to book a holiday cottage. If you see a form as an opportunity to gather information you might use at a later date, the user may object and give up. If you ask users to set up an ID and fill in a lot of personal information for a single transaction, they are likely to feel that the form is for your convenience, not theirs, and go away.

Put the items in a logical and, if possible, familiar order. If it's a long form, break it into stages and let users know where they have got to. Use as few words as possible to avoid overloading the user with instructions. Ask for only what is essential and explain why you need it. If, for example, you ask for a telephone number as well as an email address, say why. If you need information that may not be at the user's fingertips, such as a National Insurance number, tell them in advance.

Forms tend to be regarded as technical pages, as do error messages and search results, and therefore not the writer's responsibility. Although they mostly have to be created by people who know about coding, they can be considerably improved if a writer has a say in how they are worded.

The writer can ensure that technical terms such as 'populated' and 'field' stay in the code behind the page and don't appear on the page itself to baffle the user. Users mostly think they are 'filling in forms' or 'providing information'; not 'populating fields'. Why not use everyday words like 'send' and 'start again' rather than the more technical 'submit' and 'reset'? Even the term 'mandatory field', although probably familiar to many users, is unnecessary. You can say 'required information' or just 'required'. And if it's not required, why are you asking for it?

### Error messages

Uninformative error messages are some of the most infuriating pages a user can be faced with. Sometimes an error message comes up when, for example, there is a fault in the website's payment processing system, but this is not explained and users tend to think it's their fault. In fact there is nothing they can do about it except perhaps resort to the telephone, provided they can find the number.

Error messages do not have to be just '404 Page not found' or something similar; they can be as thoughtfully written as any other page. If the user has made a mistake, the error message can say what needs to be done. If the page the user wants doesn't exist, the error can offer options for where to look next, as in Figure 29. The error message should look as though it belongs to your site, with the same identifying logo or slogan and the same navigation. Then it will help retain users' confidence rather than giving

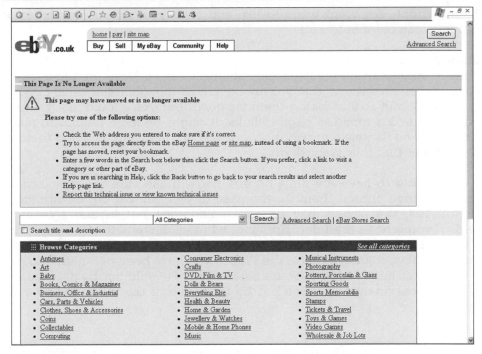

**Figure 29** A helpful error message increases users' confidence in your website.

them a fright. You want users to like and trust your site. A helpful error message can contribute a lot.

### Links pages

Links to other relevant websites are valuable to users. Encouraging users to look at other sites shows that you are confident enough in the value of what you provide not to fear losing them for good. But you should ask yourself why you need a separate page of links. It might be more helpful to place those links on the relevant pages of your site, so that users will find them at the moment that they want them.

If you decide to have the links on one page, make sure the user knows why you have chosen them. In the case of well known organizations or institutions, the names may be self-explanatory, but in many cases it helps if you write a brief description of what each website offers and why it might be useful. Otherwise it may look as though either you are just showing off your knowledge of the Web or you have been persuaded to link to a site that links to yours. Your choice of links should not be determined by reciprocal linking schemes but by the value of the other site to your users.

### FAQs

As with links pages, the question to ask yourself about Frequently Asked Questions is why you need them. The purpose of your website is to answer users' questions, so having an FAQ page suggests that you are not confident that your site is doing its job. They can be useful as a last resort, but as a user I find it irritating to go to an FAQ page and have to scroll down through lots of questions, none of which is the one I want to ask. I think FAQs, and perhaps links pages too, belong to the early days of the Web when websites were new to most people, and nothing like as sophisticated and well thought-out as they are today.

**Checklist**

- Every page on your site should be as well written as you can make it.
- Put the most important information first.
- Visualize your users and engage them as if in conversation.
- Write specific, informative links; avoid 'Click here'.
- Give users a reason before you suggest they do something.
- Write a specific <title> for every page.
- Your home page must make clear who you are, what you are offering and how to get it.
- Refer to the navigation: make the text support the links.
- It is a mistake to ask for information or commitment from a user straight away.
- Write story pages with the most important information first.
- Break transactions into stages and let users know where they are.
- Allow users to focus on the task; remove all unrelated information.
- Ensure that forms have a specific purpose and use as few words as possible.
- Write helpful error messages.
- If you have a links page, explain why you have chosen those links.
- Ensure your website answers users' questions, so that you don't need FAQs.

# Writing for search engines

Here we look at one of the main peculiarities of writing for the Web – having to write not only for the user of your site, but for potential users who are searching the Web. This chapter concentrates on what you as a writer can do to help search engines find your website, which includes being aware of the code behind your pages. Some of the advice also applies to making your site accessible to users with disabilities.

Everything in this chapter comes with a warning that search engines can change their policies at any time and render worthless any advice given here.

The interests of search engines may not coincide exactly with those of website owners, but I start by assuming that search engines want to produce the most accurate and useful results they can. It follows that we should do what we can to help them.

When people talk about optimizing their sites for search engines (Search Engine Optimization or SEO) they often mean paying search engines or exploiting technical loopholes to get their sites high up in search results. This means spending a lot of money and time monitoring their site's results in search engines, and making frequent and sometimes substantial technical adjustments that do nothing for the user. I prefer to take the long-term view and to believe that it is in the search engines' interest to reward sites that are honest, well organized, informative and fresh. You still need to monitor your site's results, but you can focus your efforts on producing good content and presenting it as best you can.

### Users' words and phrases

When you are planning your site, or a section or an individual page, imagine the kind of person you hope will find your site and think what words and phrases they might enter into a search engine. Put yourself in their position, not knowing anything about your site, just thinking of themselves and what they want. Jot down the key words and phrases that you think they might use, and try to incorporate them into your text.

This can be demanding. If, for example, you are a marketing person for a company making widgets, you want to promote your particular brand of widgets called Whizzo. The problem is that users may know only the generic term 'widget'. So you need to make sure that your text includes both 'widget' and 'Whizzo'. You may also find that using these key words and phrases does not produce very elegant copy. As a writer, you want to find original ways of appealing to the user who is reading your page; you don't want to have to cram the text with repetitions of particular words and phrases in the hope of attracting other users. You have to find a way of serving both types of user: make sure the text on your page reads well, but make sure it includes the most important words and phrases for that page.

### Hierarchy and headings

Search engines tend to give weight to what is at the top of your page. As well as putting important information first, structure your pages with a hierarchy of headings and subheadings. Try to ensure that the headings and subheadings contain important words and phrases. For example, if you are selling hairdryers write something specific such as 'How our hairdryers perform', rather than something vague such as 'Why ours are best'. Search engines look at the code behind your pages, rather than what the user sees, so use the HTML code for headings (<h1>, <h2> and so on) rather than just making them big and bold. Then search engines will recognize the hierarchy of the information on your pages.

### Links (also known as anchor text)

As links are the defining feature of a website, search engines tend to pay them quite a lot of attention. Remember that search engines look for words rather than images, so try to use significant, informative words in your links. This is yet another argument against using 'Click here' as a link (to add to those on page 168). 'Click here' is a waste of an opportunity both to provide informative links to the user and to score points with the search engines.

Your links should include words and phrases that reinforce the message on each page. Furthermore, to someone using a screen reader, 'Click here' is unhelpful because it merely tells them 'this is a link' rather than what it is a link to.

You can add information to your links in what are called 'link titles'. Link titles appear on the screen when the user puts the cursor over a link. For example, you might have a link called 'Products' which, when the cursor goes over it, shows a list of five products. They make your links more informative to the user and they may be picked up by search engines. There are problems with link titles, however. One is that if you are going to add them to your links, you probably should add them to every link in your site for the sake of consistency, and you may not want to do that. Another problem is that when a link title shows, it often obscures some other link or text, which may confuse the user. And lastly, relying on hidden text to make your message clear may mean that you make less effort to write informative links.

## Page title

I mentioned on page 174 the value of the page title (<title> in HTML) to the user who may have to wait for your page to load. The page title is also important to search engines. If you look at search results, such as those in Figure 30, you'll see that the page title is often what the search engine uses as the heading for each result. Sometimes it is only the first word, so the first word you write is more important than later words. Using a phrase like 'Welcome to the Whizzo widgets site' as the title on your home page helps to engage the user but, by starting with uninformative words, it wastes an opportunity. Each page should have a specific page title that starts with what that page is about, followed by the name of your site or organization. The title should not be too long – no more than 12 words, or about 80 characters including spaces.

## Meta data

The meta data (meaning extra information) written into the code of a Web page is read by search engines when they index websites. It is worth remembering that when people use a search engine, they are not looking at the whole Web; they are looking at the sites that the search engine has put into its index to help them find what they want. There are several different types of meta data, also known as meta tags: the important ones for writers are the <description> tag and the <keyword> tag.

You should write a specific <description> for every page. It should say what that page is about, and the words you use in the description should include words that you use on the page. What you write in your <description> is often displayed in search results, so it is an opportunity to 'sell' your site. You may use up to 200 characters – about 35 words – for the <description> but the search results are likely to display only the first 25 words, so I recommend using no more than 25, with the most important and specific information in the first 10.

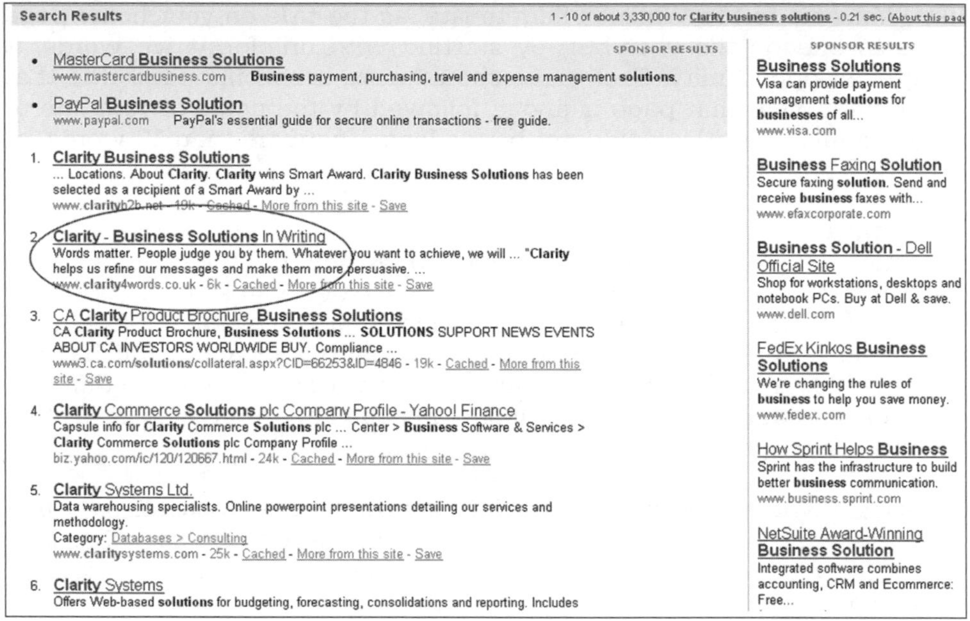


**Figure 30** Search results for 'Clarity business solutions'.

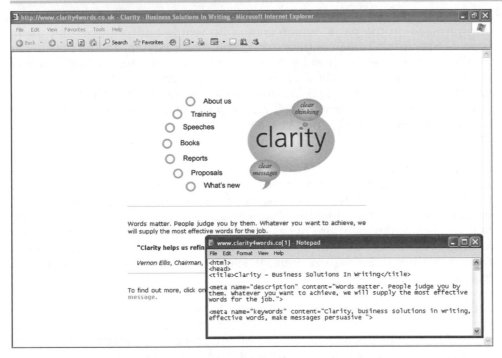

**Figure 31** Code behind 'Clarity' home page. Note how the title description and keywords appear in the search results in Figure 30.

You should use the \<keyword\> tag to include the most important words and phrases on the page, which should be words and phrases that users would enter into a search engine to find you. The \<keyword\> tag was given less weight or even ignored by some search engines after website owners abused it to put in words that they thought users would search for, but which had little or nothing to do with what was actually in their sites. It is still worth entering a few words, and especially phrases, that are central to what you are offering, but you should be careful not to repeat words, otherwise you might be penalized.

**Alternative text**

Alternative or 'alt' text is written into the code to help users who are blind or partially sighted and depend on screen readers or other devices, which cannot interpret images. Every image on a website should have 'alt' text to help make your site accessible to as many users as possible. The alternative text should convey the information that is in the image, rather than describe it. So, for example, it should say 'John Smith' rather than 'photo'.

Although it is primarily there to help people who can't or don't want to see your images, 'alt' text can be helpful to sighted users as they will read it when the cursor goes over an image. Alternative text is picked up by search engines, especially if your site contains a lot of images and not much text. Remember that search engines look for words and only recognize images that have words attached to them in the code. For all these reasons, your 'alt' text should contain significant words and phrases.

## Site map

Having a site map tends to win you favour with search engines. A clear site map, laying out the structure of your site with all the section headings and page headings, on one page if possible, is helpful to users trying to understand your site. It is also helpful to search engines because they follow links and your site map contains, or should contain, links to all the main pages in your website. It is also a good exercise for you to write out a site map, as it makes you look at your site's structure and headings all on one page, and see whether they are likely to make sense to the user.

## Fresh content

Search engines are said to love blogs (individuals' online journals) because these provide streams of fresh content every day. Search engines certainly seem to favour sites that are frequently updated. In this they are reflecting the interests of users, who like to think that they are getting the latest information and don't think much of a site that is carrying old material. This can be a problem for small sites with limited means of updating their content or for sites that are by their nature fairly static. Sites that simply provide a presence on the Web for a business or an organization (often referred to as 'brochure sites') do not need frequent updating. But even these sites can and should develop as the business or the organization develops, and as the Web becomes increasingly dominant as a means of communication.

## Checklist

- Use words and phrases that you expect people to enter into a search engine.
- Make sure the key words and phrases for each page are in the text of that page.
- Use headings and subheadings (coded <h1> etc) to show the hierarchy of information.
- Write informative links, not 'Click here'.
- Write a specific page title (<title> in HTML) for every page.
- Write a <description> for each page that includes words that are in the text.
- Write a few key words and phrases (<keywords>) in the meta data.
- Use alternative text ('alt' text) for every image and make the text informative.
- Have a site map that contains links to all your main pages.
- Produce fresh content as often as you can.

# The role of the editor

The role of the editor
The role of the editor

> The last chapter provides a variety of advice to help you maintain the quality of the site. It is based on the belief that the role of the editor is increasingly important. Web editors, or whatever they are called, must have authority over the content of the website and the means to do the job if the site is to serve the needs of the organization.

'Could you just put this onto the website for me, please?' These are words that people who look after websites have come to dread. Some authors, managers and a variety of other people seem to think that all that is necessary for their article, report or announcement to be accessible to the world is for someone to 'put it up'.

As I've argued in previous chapters, there is no point having material on a website if users can't find it or if, when they do find it, they find it unreadable. It needs to be chunked, summarized, headlined and placed in a category or section where a user would expect to find it. Someone must have the authority to rewrite or reformat material for the website or, if necessary, refuse to put it up on the grounds that it is of no value to users, at least not in its current form. I have called that person the Web editor, though he or she may work under any one of a number of job titles such as Web Assistant, Web Content Manager, Marketing Manager or Head of Communications.

Many organizations still do not have such a role. If the organization is small, it may not have the means. Even in larger organizations, there may be a person doing the website work on top of other work, or there may be several people doing bits of the work, but no single person responsible for the whole site; whereas in organizations that recognize the importance of their website, there will be a dedicated person or a team of people devoted to maintaining and developing it. What matters is that the tasks described in this chapter are done, and that the skills required to do them are valued.

### Editing

All good writers read and reread and edit their work. No-one expects to get everything right first time. Editing is a sign of strength, not weakness.

Whether you are editing your own or other people's work, do it on paper. You shouldn't be surprised by that advice. I've said all along that reading on a screen is difficult. You will edit better if you print the text and read it with pen or pencil in hand. You will also find it easier to move the pages about and compare them when you can see them all together.

Better still, get a second person to read the text as well. You are probably familiar with the material, even if you haven't written it yourself. Words that seem clear to you may not be clear to someone reading them for the first time. You may have explained something that another person finds obvious or left out something they think needs explaining. A second pair of eyes brings a fresh view. Asking for a second opinion reminds you that people understand things differently and that writing can always be improved.

Read the text through for sense. Cut out unnecessary words and find better, more concise ways of saying things. You may decide that an important piece of information is missing. You may think some ideas make better sense in a different order. You may rewrite whole chunks. If you make changes, big or small, be sure to check the text that comes before and after. Make sure that the writing flows smoothly from the old to the new and into the old again.

## Proofreading

Many people confuse editing and proofreading. They try to 'check' or 'proof' everything at once. Editing and proofreading are quite different tasks. Editing may involve substantial rewriting or even deciding not to publish something at all. Proofreading, on the other hand, is the finishing touch to text that has been edited, to make sure there are no mistakes in it. When you edit you focus on the meaning of what is written; when you proofread you focus on what is printed on the page. You need to adopt a particular attitude when you proofread. When you 'check' something, you tend to assume it is all right, but believe you ought to check it just to make sure. When you proofread, you should assume you are going to find lots of mistakes, and you usually will.

You should read the text on paper, several times if possible, and each time for a specific purpose. The more rigorously you focus on looking for one type of mistake at a time, the more likely you are to spot mistakes. Look for correct use of words, grammar, spelling and punctuation. Look particularly for words that sound the same but are spelt differently, such as 'practise' (verb) and 'practice' (noun) or 'principle' (noun) and 'principal' (usually an adjective). Look for words that are often mistyped, such as 'from' and 'form'. Look out for small words that are easy to leave out, such as 'a' or 'to' or 'for', and for redundant words that have been left in after a passage has been rewritten.

As with editing, it is a good idea to get someone else to proofread anything you have written yourself. You tend to see what you expect to see. If you have to be the proofreader yourself, try reading the text out loud; that way you are testing the words with two of your senses, not just one. You can even try reading the text backwards so that you focus on each word and don't think of the meaning at all.

### Style

Consistency is important in any publication. It is perhaps even more important on a website than in print, because users move quickly from one page to another in no particular order. They are easily thrown by inconsistencies in terminology, spelling and presentation. The Web editor should check everything that goes onto the site to make sure that consistency is maintained throughout. It helps if you make a note of words and phrases that occur frequently so that you can ensure that they appear the same way everywhere. Obvious examples are how you write dates, how you refer to your organization, what abbreviations you use, how you translate certain technical or foreign terms and so on. These notes can be the basis of a style guide for your site.

It's probably not a good idea to draw up a style guide from scratch because you may never finish the job. Several respected media organizations, such as *The Economist*, publish their style guides. Choose one of them and adapt it to your particular needs, adding style points of your own as questions arise or mistakes occur. The style of your website needs to be co-ordinated with your organization's other publications to make sure that you are speaking with one voice.

### Maintaining

A website is not a printed publication that cannot be changed once it is released. You have started a dialogue with users and they know you have the means to change your site at any time. They are intolerant of mistakes, weaknesses and out-of-date material. Maintaining a website involves constant tweaking. You should look through the pages as often as you can to see how well they read and how easy they are to use. Test them from every direction to see how they flow.

Take advantage of any opportunity to improve your site. If you give someone your Web address and you know they are going to look at your site for a particular reason, go to the relevant pages, put yourself in that person's shoes and work your way through the pages with their eyes. You will often notice something that is not as clear as it might be.

Be open to complaints and criticism; they will help you spot weaknesses in the site. If someone says your booking form is confusing, look at it again and rewrite it. It's no good if a procedure is obvious to you but not to the person it was designed for. Adapt the established commercial slogan that 'the customer is always right' and tell yourself that 'the user is always right'. If you have the means to handle it, encourage feedback. A prompt response and a positive reaction is one of the best ways of winning users' loyalty and confidence.

## Monitoring

You will normally receive statistics (log files) from your Internet Service Provider that give you all sorts of information. Look to see what search terms are being used to find your pages. This may give you ideas about what to emphasize or which new phrases to include. Try some search terms yourself and see what comes up in the results. Look carefully to see which parts of your page the search engine has picked up. Is it the <description>, the navigation or the first paragraph of your text? Put your pages through a meta tag analyzer to help you make the best use of the meta data.

If you have detailed statistics and the means of analyzing them, you can see which pages get most attention and which get least or none at all. This will help you focus your efforts on the pages that seem to be most valued by users. At the same time, it may give you ammunition to suggest that some sections should be pruned: even if they are someone's pet project, you can argue that if no-one is looking at them they should be dropped. It's not enough simply to pass on statistics. They need to be interpreted and reported in a way that makes sense to other people in the organization who may hold the purse strings. This takes time and effort.

### Developing

As the Web editor you are in a potentially powerful position because you have evidence of your users' response to what your organization is offering. Provided you are given the time and the means to make use of the information you gather, you can suggest ways in which the website and the business could develop. An organization's presence on the Web is increasingly recognized as its most important point of contact with its target audience and you are right at the heart of it.

### Using old material

One last word – recycling. The compost that enriches the Web is old material. As the Web becomes the main source of information for so many people, yesterday's words should be just as accessible as today's. This won't be relevant for all sites, and it may involve quite a lot of work, but for many sites it is worth rewriting old material or re-presenting it and making it available indefinitely.

**Checklist**

- The Web editor must have authority to rewrite material or refuse to put it on the website.
- Edit text on paper and get a second person to read it too.
- When you proofread, assume you are going to find lots of mistakes.
- Check for omissions, repetition, redundant words and mistakes in grammar or spelling.
- Ensure a consistency of style between pages.
- Test your pages on screen from every direction.
- Make use of feedback and log files to improve and develop your site.
- Use the website as a source of ideas for developing the organization.
- Recycle old material to enrich your site.

# Sources

**Books**

Max Atkinson, *Our Masters' Voices* (Routledge, 1984)

Ian Brookes & Duncan Marshall, *Good Writing Guide* (Chambers, 2004)

Tony Buzan, *Use Your Head* (BBC Books, 1974)

David Crystal, *The Stories of English* (Penguin, 2005)

The Economist, *The Economist Style Guide* (Profile Books, 2001)

Sir Ernest Gowers, *The Complete Plain Words* (HMSO/Penguin, 1973)

Wynford Hicks, *Writing for Journalists* (Routledge, 1999)

Crawford Kilian, *Writing for the Web* (Self-Counsel, 1999)

Steve Krug, *Don't Make Me Think* (New Riders, 2000)

Patrick J Lynch & Sarah Horton, *Web Style Guide* (Yale University Press, 1999)

Robert McCrum, Robert McNeil & William Cran, *The Story of English* (Faber and Faber/BBC Books, 1986)

Rupert Morris, *The Right Way to Write* (Piatkus, 1998)

Steve Morris, *Wired Words* (Prentice Hall, 2000)

Jakob Nielsen, *Designing Web Usability* (New Riders, 1999)

Office of Investor Education and Assistance, *A Plain English Handbook* (Securities and Exchange Commission, 1998)

B A Phythian, *Teach Yourself Correct English* (Hodder Educational, 2003)

Steven Pinker, *Words and Rules* (Phoenix, 1999)

Reader's Digest, *The Right Word at the Right Time* (The Reader's Digest Association, 1985)

Louis Rosenfeld & Peter Morville, *Information Architecture for the World Wide Web* (O'Reilly, 1998)

David Meerman Scott, *Cashing in with Content* (CyberAge Books, 2005)

Tom Stoppard, *The Real Thing* (Faber and Faber, 1982)

William Strunk, Jr & E B White, *The Elements of Style* (Allyn and Bacon, 2000)

Ted White, *Broadcast News Writing, Reporting and Producing* (Focal Press, 1996)

Jason Whittaker, *Producing for the Web* (Routledge, 2000)

## Articles

Bryan Magee, 'Sense and Nonsense' in *Prospect* (February 2000)

Peter Morville, 'Ambient Findability' in *Online* (November/December 2005)

George Orwell, 'Politics and the English Language' in *A Collection of Essays* (Harcourt Brace, 1981)

Nicholas Thompson, 'Sex on the Net' in *Prospect* (January 2001, originally published in *The Washington Monthly*)

## Websites

alistapart.com
cib.uk.com
freepint.com
gerrymcgovern.com
google.co.uk/webmasters
icthub.org.uk
marketingprofs.com
netmechanic.com
optimum-uk.com
plainenglish.co.uk
poynter.org
searchenginewatch.com
useit.com
webdesign.about.com
webpagecontent.com
WebPagesThatSuck.com

## Broadcasts

Melvyn Bragg, *The Routes of English* (BBC Radio 4)
Melvyn Bragg, *Do You Know What You're Saying?* (BBC Radio 4)
Jonathan Freedland, *The Long View: Trial by Jury* (BBC Radio 4)

# Index